"This helpful
human respon
selves as natura
old urge of esc
He then offers _ ....uw to exercise
courageous dependence on Christ in the midst of despair and
disappointment."

Christine Chappell, Author of *Help! I've Been Diagnosed
with a Mental Disorder*; outreach director and *Hope + Help
Podcast* host, Institute for Biblical Counseling & Discipleship; ACBC certified biblical counselor

"No matter who we are or what we experience, we're all
tempted toward escape to deal with the hurts and difficulties
of life. In this insightful book, Rush Witt gently confronts our
errant beliefs and wisely counsels our hearts to look to Jesus,
the only truly safe place to hide."

Paul Tautges, Senior Pastor, Cornerstone Community
Church, Mayfield Heights, OH; author of *Anxiety: Knowing
God's* Peace and *A Small Book for the Hurting Heart*

"When trials or temptations threaten, we feel the temptation to
escape reality. If we follow this impulse away from God, we will
only find more pain and suffering. But if we allow it to push
us toward God in faith, we can trust that he will care for us. *I
Want to Escape* provides simple, practical, gospel-centered help
to courageously trust God in the face of adversity."

J. Garrett Kell, Pastor, Del Ray Baptist Church

"This book instructs us how to turn away from fleshly escapist
responses to our troubles (which only make things worse) and
to embrace wise biblical solutions (which bring hope). Realistic
case examples are provided and Scripture is helpfully applied."

Jim Newheiser, Professor of Counseling and Pastoral
Theology, Reformed Theological Seminary, Charlotte, NC;
executive director, The Institute for Biblical Counseling
and Discipleship

"God created human beings to seek and find peace in relationship with him. Sin separated us from him and destroyed that
peace. Ever since the fall, mankind has sought after that peace,

but we too easily settle for much less. *I Want to Escape* is a wonderful, concise look at how we seek relief from the trials of life through temporary pleasures and points us to what our hearts were created for: peace with God through communion with him."

Curtis Solomon, Executive Director, Biblical Counseling Coalition; program coordinator for Biblical Counseling, Boyce College

"Sometimes life is just so very hard and it seems there is no relief from the pain, stress, and trouble. If you are here or know someone who is here, this wonderful little book will be a balm to your soul. Rush Witt reminds us of a comforting truth: Jesus is not only our Savior and Lord, he is also the Good Shepherd who is with us in our distress. The one who understands suffering, abandonment, loneliness, and tragedy can meet us in our deepest needs. You don't have to carry your burden alone. These words help you hear and listen to the One who loves you."

Daniel Darling, Director, Land Center for Cultural Engagement; best-selling author of *The Characters of Christmas*, *The Characters of Easter*, and *The Dignity Revolution*

"Amid the many ways we wrongly escape life's problems, God promises his way—not to escape the problems but the sins they might occasion. Reminding us that our Savior fights 'in the foxhole' with and for us, Rush Witt skillfully and practically outlines God's way to face life: humbly pray, freshly believe the gospel, and act boldly in dependence on him."

Robert D. Jones, Biblical Counseling Professor, Southern Seminary; author of *Pursuing Peace* and *The Gospel for Disordered Lives*

"Insightful, practical, Scripture-driven, and hopeful, *I Want to Escape: Reaching for Hope When Life Is Too Much* provides keen observations about a pervasive problem and asks questions that draw out the reader's heart. Rush Witt repeatedly reminds us that Christ is present in our current struggles, giving us the courage to engage our troubles rather than escape them."

Darby Strickland, Faculty and counselor, CCEF; author of *Is it Abuse?*

I WANT
TO ESCAPE

REACHING FOR HOPE WHEN
LIFE IS TOO MUCH

Rush Witt

New
Growth
Press

newgrowthpress.com

New Growth Press, Greensboro, NC 27401
newgrowthpress.com
Copyright © 2022 by Rush Witt

Cover Design: Studio Gearbox, studiogearbox.com
Interior Design and Typesetting: Gretchen Logterman

ISBN: 978-1-64507-275-1 (Print)
ISBN: 978-1-64507-276-8 (eBook)

Library of Congress Cataloging-in-Publication Data on file

Printed in the United States of America

29 28 27 26 25 24 23 22   1 2 3 4 5

CONTENTS

Chapter 1

I'VE GOT TO GET OUTTA HERE!

Temptation may even be a blessing to a man when it reveals to him his weakness and drives him to the almighty Savior.
— F. B. Meyer

When life overwhelms, we often want to get away—escape holds a powerful allure amid hard times. In every season, a myriad of pressures, challenges, regrets, and disappointments ooze from the ground of this fallen world and into our lives. These trials and tribulations provoke us to cry, "I've got to get outta here!" Have you felt it? Have you said it? Have you screamed it? Of course you have, and I have too. When darkness falls on us, escapism surges. We come from a long line of escapers, beginning with our first parents who hid from God in the garden (Genesis 3:8).

THE LONGING TO ESCAPE

As I type these words, I want to escape. A nasty virus has swarmed the earth. Racial tensions are exploding in the streets of our town. Conflict between Christians over masks and social distancing and vaccines and government restrictions have boiled over in the melting pot of our church. All of this has been stacked on top of the ordinary pressures of life. No one wonders why depression rates are rising along with substance abuse and even suicide. We all long to escape, and for good reason.

But even though we have many good reasons to desire escape, our faith in Jesus reminds us that we have even better reasons to depend courageously on our Savior in the ups and downs of life. And that's what this book is all about: learning to courageously depend on Christ when we yearn for escape. In the time we spend together in this book, we have three goals.

1. We wish to gain a better understanding of why escape appeals to us. Why are we so good at running for the door when life gets hard? Courageous dependence on Christ will come more quickly if we understand why escape feels so compelling.

2. We must learn to draw near to Jesus, who remains closer than a brother (Proverbs 18:24). Even when we're ready to run, even when we do run away, he relentlessly pursues his people. He won't be put off or put out by our pleas for escape. Instead, he draws close to us with grace and mercy to comfort us and lead us in the better path. His enabling grace empowers us to endure hardship when we courageously depend on him.

3. We need practical plans to shape our response to trouble. In Christ, we have a wealth of resources to help us exercise courageous dependence when life gets hard. You and I need a clear strategy to help us walk forward with Jesus, step by step.

I pray God will give us courage and comfort as we explore the reasons we so often want to run and his hope-filled direction to a better path. To my fellow escapees: Welcome—you're not alone. We're in this together. And most importantly, Jesus walks with us.

TOGETHER WITH JESUS IN OUR TROUBLE

We must remember that we struggle *together* as fellow sinners and sufferers. We are not alone because we all sin and we all suffer. But our ultimate hope and comfort comes from knowing that another Person is present in our trouble. The Lord himself has come down, entered our world, understood our need, and given us his enduring answers. At the very center of Christian courage stands not a principle or system but a Person, and this Person not only created the universe but intimately knows and loves each one of us.

As a pastor who practices premarital and marriage counseling, it's a joy to watch couples become real people to each other. Most couples begin their relationships by putting one another on pedestals. In the early days, they think they know each other, but actually the relationship hovers in a kind of unreal realm. But with time, care, and experience, something amazing occurs. They come down from their ethereal pedestal and become real people to each other. They really get to know each other. They learn the deeper details of their personalities and likes and dreams. What's happening to them in the course of their relationship through the good times and bad times? They're becoming real to each other.

We all need the same experience to dawn on us in our daily spiritual life with Jesus. Jesus Christ is the Person most present in our trouble. He has come down to really know us and to be known by us; to save us, to help us, to bless us, to carry us. Jesus is our ultimate help. By grace he endured the cross for us, and by courageously trusting in him, we find the power we need to endure when we want to escape. From this point on, I want you to intentionally think on the ever-present Person of Jesus. Let's make a habit of knowing he is near.

THREE STORIES

In this book, we hope to get much more acquainted with our own hearts and the desire inside us to escape from hard things. The good news is that we're in this together—all of us look for escape at different times and in different ways. For instance, consider the following stories of three people who dealt with a difficult situation by trying to escape. How does it work out for them? How does it work out for you?

1. The Student

Jake's dad works for an iron mill. A new and better job brought his family to a new and better town. Moving to a different city can be hard on any kid, but Jake found the transition to a new high school during his sophomore year especially difficult. Jake struggled to keep up with this school's academic rigor. Instead of changing his study habits, Jake found an easy escape online. Day after day Jake ignored his homework piling up and went to his room, put on his headphones, and played video games. When his parents tried to talk to him, he just ignored them. While he was playing video games, his only worries were about his score, and that's the way he wanted to keep it. Meanwhile, midterm grades were coming out in only a week....

2. The Lovebird

Mia and Trevor started dating two years ago. She liked his sense of humor, and he loved her wit. Talk of marriage sprang up quickly. But now a year and a half later, Trevor still hasn't popped the question. The exciting plan to build a life together is now a fading memory. Truth be told, Mia and Trevor argue more than talk, and Mia fears her dream of marriage is slipping away. She feels trapped in a relationship that is headed nowhere. Overwhelmed by daily life, Mia trades the feelings of sorrow for another feeling: pain. In the solitude of her private moments, she cuts herself. The blade stings but comforts. If she can't control her future with Trevor, at least she can control this. To her friends, cutting doesn't make sense, but to Mia, it is her escape.

3. The Patient

Terminal. It was the word Carson thought he was ready to hear, but his heart sunk deeper with each syllable. His doctors suspected cancer after Carson's first appointment, when he described having relentless headaches, fatigue, blackouts, and debilitating vertigo. Doctors gave Carson only months to live. Even so, the fear of increased pain, loss of freedom, and a mounting sense of sorrow loomed large. During his treatments, Carson met many patients who had received the same news. Some of them fixed their minds on bucket lists and final adventures. But Carson couldn't silence the panicked refrain of his heart: run, run, run. *Where can I run?* he thought. He had no place to go and not enough energy to run, so instead he binged on TV shows. He found season after season to watch (some he had seen before). Somehow watching other people's stories brought him a bit of relief—it distracted him from his story.

Jake, Mia, and Carson feel trapped by trouble. They each have their own escape routes. Each of them finds some quick relief from trouble with their preferred way of escape. But with the short-term relief comes long-term trouble. Almost anything can function as an escape route— humans are endlessly inventive about ways to escape trouble in the short term. There is shopping, gaming, watching TV, sex, pornography, sleep, sports, eating, exercising,

reading, alcohol, drugs, cutting, and even thoughts of suicide. You can probably add to this list. What does your list
include? Take a moment and think about how you deal
with trouble. What is your preferred short-term path to
relief? And what long-term trouble might be coming your
way because of it?

THE BIBLICAL, BETTER WAY

When life overwhelms us, we often see escape as our only
option. But through Scripture, God welcomes us to walk
his better way: the way of grace-enabled, faith-directed,
Christ-centered, Word-delivered, glory-focused dependence on God. I know, that's a mouthful! But over the
coming chapters, we will unpack this full-orbed view of
God's help in our trouble and apply it to life in meaningful
ways. But before we embark, I want to share one simple
verse to illuminate our way forward and help drive our
transformation from those who escape to those who courageously depend on Jesus. "No temptation has overtaken
you that is not common to man. God is faithful, and he
will not let you be tempted beyond your ability, but with
the temptation he will also provide the way of escape, that
you may be able to endure it" (1 Corinthians 10:13).

First Corinthians 10:13 has comforted my heart
in times of trouble, strengthened my grip on God, and
directed my life in countless ways. Through it we realize
our trouble is common, our God is faithful, and that courageous dependence is the way toward peace and rest. While
we naturally pursue escape routes on our own terms in our
own strength, God offers us true escape by depending on
his faithful care in the midst of trouble. Rather than giving
up and running away, we can find real refuge in God's

loving control of our lives. Instead of escaping our trouble by running from God, we can "escape" overwhelming trouble by running to God. God knows that you need to escape but not by using your own methods. Instead he offers himself so that you can endure. When we depend on God in the midst of real trouble, he will give us the courage to trust him and to give up our own methods of escape. That's what courageous dependence on God looks like.

The language of courageous dependence may seem new to you, but it's as old as the world. From the beginning of creation, every creature has been built for dependence. By our very nature, we creatures need our Creator. Every good thing we have comes from him (James 1:17). But through our fall into sin, every human heart has turned away from ultimate dependence on God. We have gone our own way, leading us into many struggles and heartaches. But we have hope in Christ. He calls us to turn back to him. Turning to Jesus instead of our usual methods of escape means we need the courage of Jesus's ever-present help—left to ourselves we will always choose to run. But Jesus is faster, stronger, and kinder than we think. He calls us back and shows us a better way forward. It all starts with turning to him.

I want you to think of the many challenges in your life, but instead of shrinking back through your chosen method of escape, you grow forward in courage, love, and purpose. Can you grow to your full potential as the person God intends for you to be without giving up your escape routes? The Bible says no. And I am guessing that deep down inside, you know the answer is no too—running away will only stunt your growth. But how do you change? How do you learn a better way—to cling tightly to Jesus instead of clinging to all those things that promise only a bit of short-term relief but in reality produce long-term trouble?

Jesus offers his people an infinitely better way than finding our own methods of escaping the troubles of life. As we depend on his help, we can replace our natural desire to escape with a courageous dependence on God, who lovingly controls our lives. By growing in this important area of the Christian life, we can find the hope and help we need to thrive under God's care for us, as he walks with us through the hard places of life. This is the better way!

REAL CHANGE

God uses a number of words in the Bible to describe his better way. Of those numerous words, *repentance* always jumps out at me. I long thought of repentance as a kind of dirty word, filled with shame and regret. But I've come to see the beauty of this incredible gift, which brings the best kind of change to our lives. Let's explore the meaning of repentance to understand the wonderful hope of a new way forward that God offers to you and me.

To quote the Puritan Thomas Watson's definition, "Repentance is a grace of God's Spirit whereby a sinner is inwardly humbled and visibly reformed."[1] The word *reformed* means changed. That's what we want! We want to be changed, and repentance is how we begin and continue to change. But also notice the two dimensions: an inward dimension and an outward dimension. One dimension is rooted in the heart, and the other is revealed in the fruit we bear. Let's be sure to keep both in view as we continue unpacking biblical change.

Perhaps like me, you also hear the word *repentance* in a harsh tone: "Suck it up, Buttercup. Stop whining and get with God's program!" Let's set the record straight by considering three attributes of real change.

1. Soul-Comforting Change

Many of your attempts to change might leave you feeling like a disobedient dog skulking back to his bed, scolded by an exasperated master. Or perhaps you feel like a child being forced to sit in the hall and think about what you've done. Change and repentance, if not properly understood, seem dreary. But true change—understood in the light of God's grace—comforts us by recentering our focus and hope on Christ, who loves us more than we know.

2. Mind-Renewing Change

God's grace transforms our minds. Paul urged his Roman brothers and sisters to resist the pull of the world by being "transformed by the renewal of your mind" (Romans 12:2). Though sin and the challenges of life can cloud our eyes and hold out our own ways of escape as the best way forward, God's gracious work of change restores our vision. Through faith, we gain the ability to see his enduring love, his patience, his nearness to us in all times. We need this vision more than the air we breathe.

During a recent trip to California, I stayed in a beautiful city surrounded by a ring of exquisite mountains. But because smog had settled into the valley, I couldn't see the mountains. When I looked out at the horizon, I thought it was just an endless sky. Because my vision was clouded, I missed the mountains' glory. Then one day the winds shifted, the smog cleared, and the mountains came into view. What a sight! In a way, our spiritual life often seems like this. Our minds are clouded by our own desire to avoid difficulty, by the world around us encouraging us to do what we can to escape trouble, and by the evil presence in our world that is always working to cloud our minds from knowing God. But we can ask for the wind of the Spirit to come and clear our vision and renew our mind. Turning to God for grace and forgiveness is the first step toward a clear mind and a clean heart. Then, Jesus enables us to draw ever closer to him as he changes us over time.

3. God-Gifted Change

Finally, we must remember real change is a gift—a soul-comforting, mind-renewing gift of grace. Especially when we feel we cannot go on, God's grace alone is what will sustain us. Just think of what Jesus Christ endured to bring us the hope and change we need! Until we personally see his nail-scarred hands, we will undervalue this magnificent gift. Knowing it comes as a gift draws us into participating in God's gracious work in our lives, like a moth to a flame.

OUR BASIC PLAN

Throughout the coming chapters, we will consider a basic plan to help us enjoy God's work of change as we stick to this biblical, better path of courageous dependence on God.

Pray with Humility

First, turn to God in prayer. With the psalmist, we cry,

I lift up my eyes to the hills.
    From where does my help come?
My help comes from the Lord,
    who made heaven and earth. (Psalm 121:1–2)

Through prayer, we can and should pour out our hearts (even our frustrations and fears) before the Lord. Like storm-tossed sailors frantically battening the hatches on the high seas, we forget the Lord who controls the winds and waves. Or even worse, we turn against the Lord—rather than to him—when we need him most. So we first must cry out to the Lord, who is our ultimate help in desperate moments. What a comfort we have in knowing—in Christ—his ears remain ever-opened and listening for our cry.

Believe with Gospel Hope

Second, put all of your faith in who God says he is. Throughout his Word and world, God has revealed to us his eternal power and divine nature (Romans 1:20). If we are not persuaded of his power, plans, wisdom, and count-less good gifts, our hearts will find no secure place to rest in times of trouble. An overwhelming desire to escape will settle in, unless we turn to the Lord for help and remind ourselves of his enduring truths. We must think carefully, deeply, and intentionally about how God's Word applies to the trials that tempt us to escape. As our belief and trust grow, our confidence in God follows. And our confidence in God will drive us cheerfully closer to him.

Act with Courageous Dependence

Third, we must act on the truth we've come to know by prayer and careful thought. In the words of the apos-tle James, God calls us to "be doers of the word, and not hearers only, deceiving yourselves" (James 1:22). For if we merely hear God's Word and not obey what he says, then we will be as the amnesiac who forgets even what he has come to know by heart. The wonderful Puritan Matthew

Henry encourages us to "Let the word of truth be carefully attended to, and it will set before us the corruption of our nature, the disorders of our hearts and lives; and it will tell us plainly what we are."[2] We are people whom God adopted as children into his family, called to be imitators of our elder brother Jesus Christ, which means, among other things, joyfully enduring our trials and temptations with him and for him and through him.

Keep this plan in mind as you read. We will look more closely at the plan in the next chapter and, through the rest of this book, apply it to life.

QUESTIONS FOR REFLECTION

1. List some ways that you try to escape uncomfortable or overwhelming situations or problems.

2. What are some of the long-term consequences you (or others) have experienced by looking for your own ways to escape?

3. What differences do you see between your natural ways of escaping the hardship and the way God offers us escape through courageous dependence on him?

PERSONAL APPLICATION

Over the course of the next forty-eight hours, take note of situations in which you have a choice between seeking your own path of escape from hard things and trusting God to walk with you through challenges. Pay attention to what you want. Do you believe that God will help you endure the hard moments, or do you just wish to escape? You might find yourself somewhere in the middle. No matter where you are, take note of how the desire for escape shapes your responses to life.

Chapter 2

WHAT ARE THE COMMON ESCAPE ROUTES?

When the wind blows cold he always takes the bleak side of the hill. The heaviest end of the cross lies ever on his shoulders. If he bids us carry a burden, he carries it also.

— Charles Spurgeon

Daring escapes fascinate me. And why not? Escape plays a key role in most great stories. The hero falls into peril, the tension mounts as all seems lost, and just in the nick of time, a climactic escape occurs. Indiana Jones slides through the booby-trapped passage, straining backward to snatch his dusty, wide-brimmed hat. Princess Buttercup escapes the clutches of Prince Humperdinck moments before she's forced to become *The Princess Bride*. Hansel and Gretel apply their own cunning to avoid the witch's oven and escape with her jewels in tow.

As Christians, escape marks major moments in the story of our faith. Israel escaped from Pharaoh, Joseph from Potiphar's wife, and Daniel from the lion's den. Peter and Paul escaped from prison on multiple occasions. And down through the ages, every person who has faith in Christ will escape the worst peril of all, God's wrath for sin. The miraculous escapes sprinkled throughout Scripture and life are given by God as wonderful gifts!

I'm grateful for them. But I've also seen and experienced the ugly side of escape.

When I look back upon my life, I find countless examples of escape gone wrong. Running away is often my first instinct when trouble comes. But like you, I feel the need to better understand my heart's obsession with escape. And like you, I want to trade my escapism for courageous dependence on God. Thankfully, by the grace of God, we can be changed from people who run from trouble to people who rest in Christ when trouble comes.

Our hearts are often fearful—always on watch, ever ready to run. If you and I can gain a keener understanding of why we struggle to trust God in our hard times, we can learn to go to Jesus, ask him for help, and he will change us! Let's explore now where our tendency to craft our own escape plans began and why it persists.

THE FALLEN SOURCE OF OUR ESCAPISM

To gain a better sense of our struggle, we must look back to the place where our love of escape began: the garden of Eden. Our first parents—Adam and Eve—were close to God and each other, perfectly good and happy when evil entered the garden. Using flattery and lies, the serpent Satan enticed Adam and Eve to break God's loving command not to eat the fruit of one special tree. For their own guilty pleasure, the first two of God's children rebelled against him, plunging themselves and their descendants into sin and darkness. It was then and there that escapism was born. "And they heard the sound of the LORD God walking in the garden in the cool of the day, and the man and his wife hid themselves from the presence of the LORD God among the trees of the garden" (Genesis 3:8).

After falling for Satan's lies, Adam and Eve heard God walking in the garden. I imagine they felt shame and guilt, uncertainty and fear; perhaps they thought they could fix their sin problem in their own strength. You and I face these distressed feelings from time to time as well. We, too, feel the relentless temptations of the world, the flesh, and the devil. Do you know what they did?

- Did they fall before the Lord with dependent hearts, pleading his compassion?
- Did they cry out from across the garden, "Father, we're here! Help us!"?
- Did they courageously run to him for comfort and restoration?

Adam and Eve took none of these good paths. Instead, they chose to hide from their troubles. Our first parents took their place as the original escapists, and original sin planted deep within us a dark proclivity for escape. Like a couple of mice concealed behind toothpicks, they crouched behind the trees. Could they really hide themselves from the presence of the all-seeing Lord God? The answer seems obvious enough. And yet we often do the very same. Going our own way instead of God's is now in our DNA as well. We, too, prefer to flee *from* God's help, rather than run *to* him for help.

Learning to go God's way instead of our escapist ways is a lifelong project, which starts with uncovering the beliefs and desires within our hearts that drive us to escape. It might be hard to see the truth about ourselves, but how else will we change and grow? As the author of Hebrews tells us, the discipline that leads to change often seems unenjoyable in the moment. But in the end, a commitment to grow our dependence on God will yield peaceful and righteous fruit (Hebrews 12:11).

I know the idea of examining yourself might be enough to put you to flight. You may even be tempted to shut this book and run. Please don't! Turn the page, keep reading, and you will find a healthy dose of hope and help as you grow into a person who runs to God for safety and strength.

THE PROBLEM IN TWO DIMENSIONS

In order to develop a courageous dependence on God, we must gain a clear view of the two-dimensional problem we face in our desire for escape. The Bible includes many places where we can learn about depending on God when temptations and trials come. But we will focus on only one. "No temptation has overtaken you that is not common to man. God is faithful, and he will not let you be tempted beyond your ability, but with the temptation he will also provide the way of escape, that you may be able to endure it" (1 Corinthians 10:13).

These sympathetic words come to us from the apostle Paul, a man well-acquainted with sin and temptation. He understood our mutual plight. Notice how he described temptation as "common to man." It means none are exempt; we all feel the effects of the fall. There is no place in this broken world where temptation cannot grow.

Another important feature we should observe in this passage is the word Paul used to talk about this common struggle to trust God. The Greek word *peirasmos* in 1 Corinthians 10:13 holds two meanings in the New

Testament. On the one hand, *peirasmos* can be translated with the word "temptation" (as it is here). On the other hand, *peirasmos* can also be translated as "trial." So the troubles we face in this life may serve two distinct functions: as temptations to fight or trials to endure. As we experience the spiritual trials that are common to us all, the difference often lies in the disposition of our hearts. If our hearts are set upon love for Christ, these spiritual challenges function more as trials, which further strengthen us through endurance. But even when our hearts are closely united to Christ, trials may function as temptations, luring us further away from our powerful Savior and tempting us to seek escape through our own power.

As we walk through life in this fallen world, we often face temptations and trials on every side. How concerning! And yet, there is good news. Not only are our temptations and trials common to man, but in Christ there is also a common answer. First, the tempting forces in this fallen world cannot operate beyond what God permits. "God is faithful," Paul wrote, and he "will not allow you to be tempted beyond what you are able." Charles Spurgeon related the restraining power and wisdom of God to the high-water mark on a shipping vessel. "The tide of temptation will rise to the high-water mark, and then God will say, 'This far you may come and no farther; here is where your proud waves halt' (Job 38:11)."[1] Second, in addition to his loving restraint, God also provides abundant and powerful resources to carry us through the fray. Paul goes on to say that when we are tempted, God "will also provide the way of escape, that you may be able to endure it" (1 Corinthians 10:13). God's way of escape is so much different than ours—and so much better! His way involves turning to him in faith and asking for the strength, help, and endurance that we need. His way means that we ask him to deliver us and look for our deliverance from him. Our hope for fighting and overcoming temptation is not anchored in our own willpower, determination, or strength. Our ability to endure trials comes not from us. Our help comes from God who controls all things—including the tempting and trying forces of this fallen world.

FOUR ESCAPE ROUTES

Let's explore four common ways we seek to escape rather than trust God in the ways that Paul described in 1 Corinthians 10:13. As you read, carefully think about how you have struggled with each one. Like me, you likely will see yourself (at least a little, and maybe a lot) in each one. Once we have a basic sense of each one, we'll take time later to dig deeper into each of them.

1. Denial

If you have ever tried to sweep your problems under a rug, you're in good company. Truly! Most people I know regularly hear the white knuckles of fear rapping on the door of their hearts. Even Christians who seem to have a rock-solid faith in God can become discouraged when temptations grow and trials persist. Despite biblical instructions to renew our courage through God's powerful grace, we can respond by pretending that everything is just fine. And we work diligently to keep up the façade and stay in denial. Though we pretend all is well, reality remains full of trouble. The choice of living in denial casts on us a self-deception. But there is a better way.

2. Distraction

Another common path to escape is distraction. When others sin against us or when a season of suffering settles upon our lives, distractions promise a reprieve. I have been known to pour myself into good endeavors, interesting hobbies, captivating entertainment, and neighborly projects. Although I love and enjoy God's many good gifts, I've also been known to use good gifts in bad ways. Can you relate? For instance, throughout my life I've struggled with procrastination. If a challenging—perhaps even undesirable—task lays ahead of me, I'm inclined to distract myself with a more enjoyable—and often less important—alternative. Or when I know a painful problem needs my attention, I allow social media to take my mind away from it. These are only a few of the many distractions I contend with in my Christian life. I imagine you have some of your own! But there is a better way.

3. Deflect and Destroy

Disappointment often holds powerful sway and influence in life, and it can provoke us to anger against people and things, even against ourselves. Both crushing defeats as well as mild letdowns seem to drag us into a pit, where we live like coiled snakes ready to bite. We deflect responsibility and declare war on those we believe have failed us. We lash out in self-destructive ways, instead of resting in God's loving care. But in reality, the worst of our troubles often do not come from other people and circumstances. They flow from our very own, unmet expectations. We place a high priority on the fulfillment of our wishes (whether consciously or unconsciously), and inevitable disappointments provoke us to walk a downward spiral of destruction. Then we end up isolated and alone, often disappointed even with ourselves. A novelist once said, "If you meet a loner, no matter what they tell you, it's not because they enjoy solitude. It's because they have tried to blend into the world before, and people continue to disappoint them."[2] It's a sobering observation. But there is a better way.

4. Death

If our destructive desires go unaddressed, they can grow into darker despair and even a desire for death. It is no wonder John Bunyan cast despair as a powerful giant in his classic story *Pilgrim's Progress*. When faced with Giant Despair, Bunyan's Christian pilgrim uses Job's words: "Brother, what shall we do? The life that we now live is miserable: for my part I know not whether is best—to live thus, or to die out of hand. 'My soul chooses strangling rather than life' (Job 7:15)."[3] God's people know what it's like to welcome death. Samson, Job, the psalmist, even Paul to some extent, all longed to depart from this world. But welcoming death as an entrance to heaven and seeing God face-to-face is different from trying to escape our troubles through our own death. That's why, of these four escape routes, despair and death are the most tragic. Fueled by discouragement, displeasure, and disappointment, despair has led some to contemplate the most final of escapes: suicide.

Despite the shocking nature of suicide, Scripture does not turn a blind eye or unfeeling heart. God's Word speaks directly to the allure of this ultimate escape, and he offers us a better hope than any the world offers. Even here, the hope of the gospel can break through the ominous clouds with rays of grace. Again, we need to know there is a better way.

Whether overwhelming circumstances tempt us to deny, distract, destroy, or even die, the God who never runs from trouble is he who holds us, his beloved children, in the palm of his sovereign, wise, and good hand.[4] We can rejoice in knowing his sanctifying work replaces our love of escape with something far, far better: a courageous dependence on God! What could be better?

BIG HOPE FOR HARD TIMES

I grew up a Nike kid. My parents bought Air Jordans for me, and I wore a neoprene sleeve on my left knee, just like Mike (I didn't have a knee injury; it was just for looks). The Michael Jordan era swept me away in a consuming passion to "be like Mike." But like every boy my age, I faced the crucial question: Be like Mike? How can I ever be like Mike, who remains the greatest of all time? Nike offered a wildly naive answer to all my dreams: "Just do it."

Just do it? Oh, okay. Sure. No problem. I'll just do it.

But an obvious problem stood in the way. I couldn't *do it*. I couldn't even *begin* to do it. No amount of time spent in the gym or the basketball court would ever turn me into Michael Jordan.

Early in my Christian life, the same feeling of inability came home to me. When facing my own sin or suffering or need for change, less thoughtful Christians sounded like Nike. They said, "Just do it." Just get better. Just cheer up. Just be brave. Just endure. I wish I knew then what I know

now. We can't *just do it*. We need help, and we need a lot of help. But I have good news! The God of the universe—sovereign, wise, and good—knows where we are, understands our incredible need for help, and he has given us in Christ everything pertaining to life and godliness (2 Peter 1:3). With that thought, we can begin to scratch the surface of God's wonderful help in Christ by seeing five qualities of the help he brings to hard lives when we depend on him.

Quality 1: Grace-Enabled Dependence

We begin by recognizing this foundational truth: even our ability to depend on God is a gift of grace. Without his grace, we would never even be able to turn to him to ask for help. All of us are living in a hard, broken world. If we are to grow in courage and faith, then we need grace above all else. The grace of Christ not only saves our souls but transforms our lives. By grace, he grants us lasting comfort, new desires, and practical tools to build our courageous dependence upon him. Simply put, when we feel our need for God's help, it is a gift of grace.

When we feel the rising urge to run, wisdom calls us to pray fervently for God to put his grace to work. For this reason, the author of Hebrews calls us to "with confidence draw near to the throne of grace, that we may receive mercy and find grace to help in time of need" (Hebrews 4:16). What a wonderful thought: you and I can draw near to the God of help! Pray right now for God to pull you close.

Quality 2: Faith-Directed Dependence

In troubling moments, we can often feel disoriented, not knowing which way to turn. But when we depend on God (which is only possible because of his grace!), he directs us by faith in Christ.

But our faith wanes when we lose heart, doesn't it? We need a regular refreshing of our faith. We need God to open our eyes to see anew the truths that may have become routine to us.

As with our plea for grace, we should pray for a deeper and wider faith in Christ. The very disciples of Jesus felt this same need as they said to Jesus, "Increase our faith!" (Luke 17:5). If they asked for greater faith, shouldn't we?

Quality 3: Christ-Centered Dependence

The reason we can have hope in hard times is Jesus Christ. He holds center position in the universe, and by faith, he holds center position in our lives. In recent years, the term Christ-centered has risen in popularity: we have Christ-centered churches and Christ-centered Bible studies and Christ-centered ministries. Any lingo can lose its luster with frequent use, but we must keep Christ-centeredness fresh. A Christ-centered dependence recognizes that real hope rests with Jesus, not with the ways we are tempted to escape, and not even ultimately with our own good deeds or healthy habits. As we continue thinking about the pull of escape, we must keep Jesus central.

The author of Hebrews exhorts us to fix our eyes on Jesus (Hebrews 12:2). Fixing our eyes on Jesus, the author and perfecter of faith, means to center our life on Christ and his love. As we explore the way to live when life overwhelms, we must remember to keep returning to the center of life—Jesus Christ, who is always with us.

Quality 4: Word-Delivered Dependence

God's help comes to us in a form that we might not expect. If you were stranded on a rocky ledge and unable to escape, what would you think if the rescue team showed up and threw you a book instead of a rope? You would be utterly confused. Your scream would echo, "What's this?" The rescuer shouts back, "Read it and you'll see. It's your only hope!"

As strange as it sounds, one of the primary ways that God helps us is through a book—the Bible. In it, he has revealed his glorious plan to redeem struggling people like us, from the muck and mire of sin, by grace alone. And not only does the Bible teach us how our souls can be saved from the consequences of sin; God's Word also gives us the all-sufficient hope and help we need in the overwhelming situations of life. It's in God's Word that we meet Jesus and hear from him. Our relationship to Christ is grounded in the Bible. His words to us deliver an endless stream of refreshing hope.

Quality 5: Glory-Focused Dependence

You've heard the phrase, "last but not least." There exists no greater "last but not least" than this fifth quality of our dependence on God. We cap off this brief list with the greatest hope of all: the glory of God. God does everything in an eternal quest for his own glory. But the incredible reality of our unity with Christ settles in when we realize that he has invited us into his glory.

In prayer, Jesus declares an incredible truth: "The glory that you have given me I have given to them, that they may be one even as we are one" (John 17:22). Do you see the astounding place of glory in God's plan? The Father gave his glory to Jesus, and Jesus has promised his glory to us, his people. Because God loves his glory, he has vowed to help us move forward with him. Therefore, in Christ, we can have a new, hopeful outlook on our own suffering and hardship. We see in them opportunities to glorify the God who cares for us (1 Corinthians 10:31)! Glory has the power to transform even the deepest, darkest trouble, fueling our courageous dependence on the God of glory.

QUESTIONS FOR REFLECTION

1. What do you love about escape? When you see a magician accomplish a feat or when an escape is written into the story line of a movie or book, what about it captivates your attention?

2. Think of a time when you didn't respond to an overwhelming moment by escaping. What did you do instead? Why did you respond in that way?

3. Consider the "Four Escape Routes" mentioned in the chapter. Which of the routes plays the strongest role in your life?

PERSONAL APPLICATION

Each day this week, spend time reflecting on and praying to God about each of the five qualities of God's wonderful help in Christ. Determine each day to find one way in which each quality connects to your daily life or the life of someone you want to love and help.

Chapter 3

THE BETTER WAY: COURAGEOUS DEPENDENCE

To learn strong faith is to endure great trials.
I have learned my faith by standing firm amid severe testings.

— George Mueller

"It's as easy as riding a bike," they say. Honestly, though, riding a bike is *not* easy. And as a father of five children, I can tell you *teaching* someone to ride a bike is twice as hard. I wish I could say we made beautiful memories in the street outside our house on those warm summer days. I can only describe it as an exercise in patience (which I repeatedly lost with each child). I resorted to threatening, pleading, and sometimes shouting—all in the name of fatherhood.

Each of my children quit no less than ten times in the course of my training. If they couldn't learn to ride without wobbling or falling or feeling foolish in the process, they gave up. A world of freedom lay ahead of them—crisscrossing streets, bike trail excursions, trips to the convenience store for Popsicles®, and alleyway adventures. But in the moment of struggle, all they felt was their natural instinct to quit, to dash back inside the house, to escape.

THREE REASONS WE CAN DEPEND ON GOD

The story of discouragement and frustration that played out in front of my house repeats over and over in daily life. We lose sight of the joy and freedom God promises through our trials. Even in our spiritual lives, courage melts away when life becomes harder than we expected. Sometimes we question if the troubles are worth the pain, and the rewards of his grace lose their appeal. We run for the exit. True spiritual growth calls for a return to God himself. Because he holds out abundant grace to overwhelmed people, he can reorient our hearts around his own sovereignty, wisdom, and goodness—a trio of enduring truth.

1. Sovereignty

Our dependence on Christ springs from our trust in God's control over all things. When God seems distant, Christians can draw strength from meditating on his ultimate supremacy.

Perhaps no Psalm packs more sovereignty into a few verses than Psalm 93. Read these powerful words:

> The Lord reigns; he is robed in majesty;
>   the Lord is robed; he has put on strength as his belt.
> Yes, the world is established; it shall never be moved.
> Your throne is established from of old;
>   you are from everlasting.

The Lord stabilizes the fallen world despite all the forces of chaos. Resting in the sovereignty of God can instill hope, joy, and confidence in God's people—even in the midst of trials and troubles. Yet hope, joy, and confidence can be so hard to come by in seasons of real trouble.

Sometimes the idea of sovereignty seems cold and controlling, as though we must simply trust that God is pulling the right levers in heaven. Personally, I've often overlooked the incredible love God exercises toward us in all his sovereign works. So to find comfort in God's sovereignty in the midst of our trials and temptations, we need to not just mentally affirm the doctrine of God's sovereign power over all of his creation. We also must meditate on his loving providence. He is not impersonally pulling levers up in heaven; he is working all things together for our good and gladness in him. Perhaps no passage of Scripture catches this truth more clearly than Romans 8:28, "And we know that for those who love God all things work together for good, for those who are called according to his purpose." This single verse has been a magnificent hope to a myriad of Christians throughout history.

Susannah Spurgeon—wife of the English preacher of the 1800s, Charles Spurgeon—found strength in knowing, "The soul that has learned the blessed secret of seeing God's hand in all that concerns it, cannot be a prey to fear, it looks beyond all second causes, straight into the heart and will of God, and rests content, because he rules."[1] As ministry challenges surged for her husband, through fire and loss, Susannah's dependence upon the sovereignty of God enabled her to support Charles in times of overwhelming grief. Without doubt, Susannah's trust in God helped steady her husband's pen as he wrote of God's loving control, "There is no attribute of God more comforting to his children than the doctrine of Divine Sovereignty. Under the most adverse circumstances, in the most severe troubles, they believe that Sovereignty hath ordained their afflictions, that Sovereignty overrules them, and that Sovereignty will sanctify them all."[2]

Spurgeon wrote these words in May 1856, five months before a false report of fire in the church building set off a stampede of people ten thousand strong. Dozens were trampled and seven died. Spurgeon was distraught, but his belief in God's loving sovereignty comforted and carried him through the rest of his ministry.

In his last sermon, Spurgeon preached of Christ who is "always to be found in the thickest part of the battle. When the wind blows cold he always takes the bleak side of the hill. The heaviest end of the cross lies ever on his shoulders. If he bids us carry a burden, he carries it also."[3] We, too, can trust God's good providence in times of trial because he is both all-powerful and all-loving.

2. Wisdom

Our dependence on Christ springs from a keen sense that God's wisdom far surpasses all human wisdom and his incredible promise to share his wisdom with us when we ask him (James 1:5). From Genesis to Revelation, the Bible declares the depths of God's wisdom. In Proverbs 8, Lady Wisdom belongs exclusively to the eternal God. She reveals the wisdom of God, and readers are exhorted to recognize her surpassing beauty and honor. She was with him from the beginning before the oceans teemed with creatures, before the mountains loomed larger than life, and before the heavens declared the glory of God. She declares in the streets God's perfect knowledge and trustworthiness. When we question God's love or decisions, even his mysterious ordination of difficult times, she assures us that God knows what he's doing, and his will cannot be improved. His wisdom comforts us and directs us to pray with humility, believe with gospel hope, and act with courageous dependence.

When I feel stuck in a cycle of escape from my problems, I simply cannot imagine a way to regain my joy except to fly away like a bird. But God's wisdom shows us how joy can be ours in the midst of trials and troubles. James 1 presents a startling view through the eyes of God: "Count it all joy, my brothers, when you meet trials of various kinds, for you know that the testing of your faith produces steadfastness. And let steadfastness have its full effect, that you may be perfect and complete, lacking in nothing" (James 1:2–4). Oh, how impossible it is for me to see this truth on my own! When I face various kinds of trials, joy often stands at the bottom of my list of priorities. I just want out. But here God tells us we can and should "count it all joy."

In order to follow God's joy-counting lead in the time of trial, we need his wisdom, so we can see why trials can be counted with joy. Only God's wisdom can show us how God, in his loving providence, grows us through the testing of our faith. For this reason, James immediately compels us, in the very next verses, to ask God for wisdom. And here's the good news—"it will be given" (James 1:5)!

3. Goodness

The goodness of God completes our trio of enduring truth. I shudder to think of living under an all-sovereign, all-wise god who lacks goodness and love. But our God is good, and in his goodness he has showered us with mercy.

Like nourishing rain that falls from the heavens and wets the ground, God's goodness fills our lives with good things. Through Christ, we can rejoice in David's comforting expectation, "Surely goodness and mercy shall follow me all the days of my life, and I shall dwell in the house of the LORD forever" (Psalm 23:6). His psalms portray a man often on the run from enemies, in constant danger, under relentless pressures. How can David say, "Your goodness and mercy are with me every day"?

With this question, we arrive at an important intersection on the river of truth. For many people, only two channels appear before them. The channel to the right says God in his goodness holds back overwhelming hardships. To the left, another channel points to a world in which hardships signal a deficiency in God's love or power. But there's good news: a third way lies between them. A stream of grace brings together the truth of God's goodness and the hard realities of life in a fallen world. How could David say, "Your goodness and mercy are with me every day," as suffering swells and enemies rage? Three words: *in his goodness*. David learned God's goodness and life's hardships do not conflict but rather complement one another. Notice in three consecutive Psalms the specific ways David learned God's goodness.

David learned God's goodness because God visits his people in their trouble.

> You have tried my heart, you have visited me by night,
>> you have tested me, and you will find nothing;
>> I have purposed that my mouth will not transgress. (Psalm 17:3)

David learned God's goodness because God listens to his people when they call.

> In my distress I called upon the Lord;
>> to my God I cried for help.
> From his temple he heard my voice,
>> and my cry to him reached his ears. (Psalm 18:6)

David learned God's goodness because God speaks to his people in his Word.

The law of the Lord is perfect,
    reviving the soul;
the testimony of the Lord is sure,
    making wise the simple;
the precepts of the Lord are right,
    rejoicing the heart;
the commandment of the Lord is pure,
    enlightening the eyes;
the fear of the Lord is clean,
    enduring forever;
the rules of the Lord are true,
    and righteous altogether. (Psalm 19:7–9)

God is present, not absent, when troubles rise. He walks with us through the losses and crosses of life. His goodness fuels our endurance. But we must submerge our hearts in the stream of God's grace. When we drift off course and lose sight of God's goodness, our escape instinct rises again.

A THREE-PART PLAN FOR COURAGEOUS DEPENDENCE

Whoever we are or whatever we face, sin tempts us to avoid suffering at all costs. Yet, in his grace, God offers us the better path we've been considering: courageous dependence on God. But we need a plan.

How should we respond to these moments of desperation? A biblical three-part plan has helped me and others to renew our hearts and minds when escape seems our only option.

1. Pray with Humility

Our plan starts with the most important (and maybe most neglected) discipline: *Pray with sincere humility*. God has given fervent, hope-filled, God-centered prayer as a powerful weapon in our fight. In times of distress—when our hearts falter under the pressures of daily responsibilities, the hardships of life, the ruling desires that captivate us, and ungodly beliefs that lead us astray—we must turn to the Lord and beg him for the help we need.

As we pray, we bring to God our overwhelming sense of weakness and, at times, even our failure to stay composed during the most trying situations. King David cried out to God this way, in Psalm 22, as he drew near to God in his time of trouble, saying, "But you, O Lord, do not be far off! O you my help, come quickly to my aid!" (Psalm 22:19). Can you hear the humility in his words? I often turn to this kind of prayer as a last resort, not a first response. I need a constant reminder to cry out to the Lord, with a humble heart, knowing he is the ultimate help in these desperate moments.

When we feel overwhelmed by hardship, our focus on prayer can wane. Just recently, I experienced a time of discouragement and despair. I struggled to know how to pray or even what words to use. In those dark moments, if you can focus on one key prayer, it might be this: *Help me cling to you*. This is precisely what humility does—it clings! Humility doesn't try to live independent of God but in utter dependence upon him. Sometimes in human relationship, we look down on clingy-ness. But in our relationship with God, nothing could be better than clinging to him. When you don't know how to pray, "Help me!" is always a good place to start.

While it's certainly good and right to set aside a time of prayer with God each day, the Scriptures envision a ceaseless attitude of prayer. Paul wrote, "Rejoice always, pray without ceasing, give thanks in all circumstances; for this is the will of God in Christ Jesus for you" (1 Thessalonians 5:16–18). He didn't mean we should close our eyes and all day pray formally. Instead, the message is the value of a prayerful disposition toward life and God, even in hard times. A prayerful attitude will help us rejoice and give thanks in all circumstances. Especially when we want to escape, we must keep prayer central. It's in prayer that we receive the courage to endure from our faithful Savior who endured for us.

2. Believe with Gospel Hope

The second part of our plan calls us to keep on believing. Children of the '80s (like me!) remember the rock band Journey's most popular song, "Don't Stop Believing." With nearly one billion plays on Spotify, the anthem still resonates with an entire generation. Journey tapped into the core of human nature by releasing a song about belief as the first track on their biggest studio album, *Escape*. Five young San Francisco rockers struck a chord by singing about the inextricable link between belief, hope, and our temptation to escape when pressures rise.

How much more can we, people who have received from God the deep wisdom of special revelation, appreciate the value of Christian belief in times of trouble! Rock and roll prophets may exhort us to "hang on to that feeling," but they can't tell us exactly what we ought to believe. God's Word, however, always speaks the truth. His Word instructs us not only *to believe* but *what to believe*.

Like the rudder of a ship, our heartfelt beliefs direct us in the stormy circumstances of God's world. As the white-capped waves of hardship surge, our beliefs will either direct us to depend on God or to look elsewhere for help. To battle against the temptation to escape, we pray for the gift of faith so that we will be filled with gospel hope. And when hope takes root, the compelling force of faith causes us to lean wholeheartedly on Christ.

You see, there is a direct relationship between what we believe and our dependence on God. If I don't believe in God's loving providence, I won't trust God's promises of protection and care. If you don't believe in God's wisdom, you won't listen carefully to his directions. If I don't believe in God's goodness, I won't rest in his fatherly compassion. The more the truth cultivates and refines our beliefs, the more we will draw near to him. Then, the closer we draw, the stronger our hope and confidence in Christ will grow.

Much the same thing is in Romans, as Paul tied endurance to God's love, which is flooded into our hearts by his Spirit. "More than that, we rejoice in our sufferings, knowing that suffering produces endurance, and endurance produces character, and character produces hope, and hope does not put us to shame, because God's love has been poured into our hearts through the Holy Spirit who has been given to us" (Romans 5:3–5). The Holy Spirit gives us the power to believe and leads us into all truth (John 16:13). It's the Holy Spirit that opens our eyes to see Jesus and to know his love, his power, and his comfort. All of the promises of God are yes and amen in Jesus. When we put all of our faith in him, we are filled with hope and given the strength to endure; when on our own, we would run for the hills.

3. Act with Dependent Courage

Finally, our three-part plan leads us to *act with dependent courage*. When the challenges of life rage around us, and we begin to dip under the whelming flood, our resolve to act flies away. Do you feel paralyzed in those moments? Something big looms on the horizon, and you just keep putting it off. Your to-do list seems to grow by the minute, and the pressure tempts you to give up and run away. By God's powerful grace, at work through our prayers and faith, we can learn to take action.

At times, I've heard obedience styled as a cold, pull yourself up by your bootstraps, *just do it* kind of thing. As a younger pastor, I foolishly tried to encourage people on to this kind of compliance. Obedience marched to the tune of a legalistic drum. No real thought, no compelling love was needed to obey, just a submissive will. Oh, how wildly I missed the target of obedience.

As Christians more thoughtful than I nurtured me in the gospel, my view of obedience became deeper, brighter, and lovelier than I ever imagined possible. Together with them, I am still waking up to the clear teaching of the Bible, which I for so long failed to understand: the love of God in Christ motivates the kind of courageous dependence that most delights God. Among many passages of the Bible, Paul's words to the Colossians stand out:

> And so, from the day we heard, we have not ceased to pray for you, asking that you may be filled with the knowledge of his will in all spiritual wisdom and understanding, so as to walk in a manner worthy of the Lord, fully pleasing to him, bearing fruit in every good work and increasing in the

knowledge of God. May you be strengthened with all power, according to his glorious might, for all endurance and patience with joy, giving thanks to the Father, who has qualified you to share in the inheritance of the saints in light. (Colossians 1:9–12)

Do you feel in Paul's words the surprising warmth of trusting God even when you feel overwhelmed and inadequate? Do you think of your obedience to Christ as being filled with knowledge and wisdom, worthy of the Lord, in every way pleasing to him, full of fresh fruit, gloriously strong in power to endure, joyously patient, and overflowing with thankfulness to the Father? As we practice together this plan—to pray with sincere humility, believe with gospel hope, and act with dependent courage—I pray God will enlarge our vision of his love in our often difficult and overwhelming lives.

HOPE FOR CHANGE

At the age of twenty-three, Dillon sensed God was calling him to a new season of education. The certification program would help him serve his local community. Soon after classes began, Dillon felt overwhelmed. The program demanded more time and attention than he had anticipated. Doubt and fear grew in his heart. Dillon found himself procrastinating on assignments, dreading the next class, and strategizing ways he could silence his sense of calling. But a day before he planned to drop out of the program, a wise friend stepped in to help Dillon pray, believe, and then act with courageous dependence. This friend reminded Dillon of the truth: God is able. He found new courage to press on toward the goal of serving God more effectively in his community.

Every person feels the temptation to escape rather than live in the enduring resources Jesus brings in the gospel. But there's good news: the resources of Jesus remain and every day, every Christian can find help to pray, believe, and act. Jesus comforts his people with the truth that in tribulations we have infinite reason to trust his powerful love. Jesus has overcome the world and walks with us in it.

With this three-part approach to our trials in mind, in the next few chapters we can move forward to consider four ways we turn to the better way of courageous dependence on God.

QUESTIONS FOR REFLECTION

1. Like children learning to ride a bike, what experiences in life most tempt you to quit?

2. Which of the three attributes of God—sovereign, wise, and good—encourage you most?

3. Which parts of the three-part plan come easiest to you? With which do you struggle most?

4. How would you describe your hope that God can change you? Are you hopeful? Do you lack hope? Why do you think you feel this way?

PERSONAL APPLICATION

Write down a list of ways God has shown you his sovereignty, wisdom, and goodness. Make this list as long as possible. Then share your list with a trusted friend. Talk together about the many ways God cares for you and how his care empowers you to endure difficult times.

Chapter 4

WHY DOESN'T DENIAL WORK?

*God uses the encouragement of the Scriptures, the hope of our
ultimate salvation in glory, and the trials that he either sends or
allows to produce endurance and perseverance.*

— Jerry Bridges

Are you living in denial? You might be if

- you have a hard time talking about difficult subjects;
- even when things go wrong, you say everything is fine;
- you invent excuses for why things are not really as bad as they may seem; or
- when other people are troubled or uncomfortable, your first instinct is to encourage being positive (with or without any evidence that everything will work out!).

LIVING IN DENIAL

In 2012, I moved from Florida to Columbus, Ohio, to plant a church a few miles from downtown. My family acclimated to the city we call home. At this point, I could see myself living nowhere else, except perhaps Denial, Ohio.

But Denial, Ohio, doesn't exist. It's only in a commercial that's part of a marketing campaign to oppose the opioid crisis in our state. In the commercial, viewers are invited to imagine Denial as a place where the residents ignore the problem of addiction running rampant on the streets and halls of their neighborhoods and schools. "Oh my kids would never use opioids. They're good kids. They would tell me if someone offered them drugs. That stuff doesn't happen here in Denial. It's a nice town."[1] The narrator's pithy response presses the warning, "Don't live in Denial, Ohio."

Every time I see this commercial, I'm forced to recognize the stinging notion that life in Denial appeals to me. The citizens live in oblivious bliss, ignoring the crisis all around them. They smile, laugh, play games, and go about their peaceful days none the wiser.

We know denying or minimizing problems solves nothing, and that fact enables the commercials to strike a nerve with viewers. Yet it doesn't keep us from seeking escape from some spiritual struggles by denying they are real or by minimizing the seriousness of the problem. Because you and I are on the path of courageous dependence on God, we must refuse to live in denial.

THE STORY OF DANA "THE DODGER"

Gather in your mind a picture of Dana. He works a high-pressure job in a busy financial investment firm. The company leaders drive their investors with an iron will. The president, Mr. Dobetter, demands excellence and profit at all cost. Each moment of Dana's workweek burns with a white-hot pressure to perform. On top of the many pressures, Dana recently received a negative annual review of his work. It seems his efforts have not helped the company reach its goals, and now Dana faces termination if his production doesn't improve within six months.

Despite the negative review and the prospect of losing his job, Dana manages not to worry. Actually he manages to not do much of anything. At the end of each day, Dana commutes home with no greater desire than for a little peace and quiet. He insists nothing is wrong. Instead of seeking help from a coworker or asking for help from his supervisor, Dana chooses to continue on with the status quo. *Somehow*, he thinks, *everything will work out*. When his wife asks him about work, he says everything is fine. He doesn't want to talk about his review or being on probation. Instead when he comes home, he retreats to his recliner, watches sports, drinks a few beers, and tries to pretend that nothing bad is happening. He stays zoned out from his coworkers, his wife, and his children. All of them can see that something is wrong; the only one who seems oblivious is Dana.

What's going on? In the pressing moments of life—like us all—Dana loses his grip on God. His eye drifts from the Father of mercies and the God of all comfort, "who comforts us in all our affliction, so that we may be able to comfort those who are in any affliction, with the comfort with which we ourselves are comforted by God" (2 Corinthians 1:4). Nevertheless, even when Dana loses his grip on grace and gets lost in denial, God does not lose his grip on Dana. As we will see at the end of this chapter, as he turns to God and admits he needs help, Dana's beliefs and desires can be changed and lead him to serve his company and family well again.

Dana chose the path of denial because it seemed easier than facing a difficult reality. He was blind to the value of adversity in his life. In his mind, the struggles at work are more of a hassle to avoid than an opportunity to embrace. Instead of ignoring trouble, Dana needs the powerful reminder that God uses our struggles to work his will in our lives.

THE VALUE OF TRIALS ENDURED

At least in part, we seek escapes from the difficulties of life because we fail to appreciate how God uses our trials to draw us close, to build our faith, and to make us more like him. Consider Jonathan Edwards, an eighteenth-century pastor who loved the gospel of grace. Edwards lived through many difficulties, but when troubles came, Edwards saw them as opportunities to embrace Christ, rather than hard realities to ignore. For twenty years, Edwards pastored a church in Northampton, Massachusetts. In 1750, 90 percent of the congregation voted to fire him. As a pastor, I can think of few experiences more painful and discouraging than seeing my church turn me out. Can you imagine the many ways Edwards could have chosen the path of denial? He could have consoled himself with the thought that next year they'd see the error of their ways and take him back, or he could have decided just to move somewhere else and pretend the heartache never happened. Instead, he responded by embracing God's loving care in the midst of the trouble, and he continued to serve God in meaningful ways.

Despite the painful disappointment of termination, he spent the next—and last—seven years of his life in ministry to the Mohawk Native Americans of Stockbridge. Edwards's belief in God's care propelled him forward in service to Christ. God used the challenges of life to develop in Edwards a theology of endurance. In his book *Religious Affections*—a Christian classic in its own right—Edwards identified a "three-fold benefit" to enduring trials. An embrace of these benefits offers us yet another tool in our exercise of endurance.

1. Trials Prove the Genuineness of Faith

The first of Edwards's three-fold benefits is that trials prove the genuineness of our faith. As fire tries and refines gold, trials refine our faith and reveal its true nature. To test its metal, the jeweler applies a flame. Pure gold will brighten in the heat, while fake pieces darken and melt.[2] In a similar way, by endurance the heat of life manifests the true commitment of our faith in Christ.

The apostle Peter exalted the value of enduring dependence on God by writing, "In this you rejoice, though now for a little while, if necessary, you have been grieved by various trials, so that the tested genuineness of your faith—more precious than gold that perishes though it is tested by fire—may be found to result in praise and glory and honor at the revelation of Jesus Christ" (1 Peter 1:6–7). Like a hand on the stove, when the heat of life burns hot, we pull back in panic. We assume the worst of our trials, as though God designed them for our demise. Peter said the opposite: God fashions our trials for good. By them, he draws out the glory of our faith as it endures by grace. So our dependence on him in these times shows the genuine substance of our faith in Christ.

2. Trials Make the Beauty of Faith Appear

The second benefit is that trials not only manifest the truth of our faith in Christ but also make faith's warm beauty shine like the sun. As our moon reflects sunlight through the darkness, trials provide a backdrop on which

Jesus's supremacy and glory glow. But to really understand God's plan to broadcast his glory through the world,
we must consider the primary way in which his disciples
shine forth.

The twelves disciples of Jesus (including Judas, the
Son of Perdition) displayed the glory of God most bril-
liantly through seasons of significant struggle. It was on
the beaten and battered backdrop of trouble that their lives
shined for him. In the soul-satisfying joy of their King,
his supremacy beamed around the globe. Or as the Puritan John Flavel insists, "Hereby the most wise God doth
illustrate the glory of his own name, clearing up the righteousness of his ways by the sufferings of his people. . . .
By exposing his people to such grievous sufferings, he gives
a fit opportunity to manifest the glory of his power . . .
and of his wisdom."[3] John Piper's mantra holds true: God
was most glorified in them when they were most satisfied
in him, even in the midst of their trials.[4] Just as Edwards
promised, the trials of the Christian need not be dreaded,
for they make the beauty of faith appear glorious. As we
draw near to Jesus, this story can become our stories.

3. Trials Purify and Increase Affection for Christ

The third benefit of trials that Edwards identified
is how they purify and increase our affection for Christ.
Seldom do we find a more sincere and lasting affection
than among war-torn soldiers. Writing about the 506th
Regiment of the 101st Airborne, who parachuted into the
European Theater of WWII, Stephen Ambrose noted how
the shared experience of enduring the war together pressed
the men into a band of brothers. He recounted, "They also
found in combat the closest brotherhood they ever knew. . . .

They found that in war, men who loved life would give their lives for them."[5] The experience of soldiers such as these casts but a shadow in comparison to the affection for Christ that can grow in the soil of adversity. Endurance through spiritual battles with Christ as the captain of our faith purifies and multiplies our love for him.

In the foxhole, we look over to see our Savior fighting with and for us.

Can you see him? His face bears the marks of a sleepless night in prayer, his back bloodied by the flogger's tassels, his hands and side scarred by crucifixion. There he stands, in glorious display of his love.

Can you hear him? As bombs explode in the field and bullets ricochet off the rocks, he speaks words of comfort and consolation and courage. He intercedes for you with divine prayers, which sustain you in the fight.

Can you feel him? As your brother in arms, he picks you up and carries you to the next waypoint. He lifts a dusty canteen to your parched lips and refreshes you with cool water. He, the truest brother in your band, battles with you in the fray, and as you see him and hear him and feel him at work in your trials, your affections for him will soar. How else could you have this if not for your trials?

FAKING PEACE

Another way the escape route of denial works against us is to lead us to live in an unreal dream. Though troubles and conflicts surround, in denial we insist all is well. *Everything is fine now. It's all fine. Just relax, and we'll have you out of here in no time.*

Tony Agpaoa practiced a fraudulent brand of medicine.[6] Until his death in 1982, he performed "psychic

surgery" on hundreds of Filipino patients. Many deteriorated and died. Psychic surgery offers healing by denial.
Patients suffering serious conditions believe doctors like
Tony will perform careful surgery, but they only perform
a cruel scam. Lain prostrate on a makeshift operating bed,
naive sufferers feel the push and pull of the doctor's hands.
If they dare to look, patients see their doctor pull out a
clump of bloody tissue, presumably the malignant tumor
that has stolen away their health. In reality, the doctor
holds a bloody lump of animal flesh, which he made
appear by sleight of hand. The fake physician pretends to
sew up the incision. *Everything is fine now. Just relax.*

Pretending to heal diseases, psychic surgeons take
their place as the chief peace-fakers of the medical community. People suffering real ailments, in need of real
help, are sold a bill of goods and told all will be well. Tragedy upon tragedy. And yet, the fraud shadows an even
greater tragedy, of a similar but spiritual kind, occurring
over and over in daily life. The allure of escape offers
peace through the denial of spiritual trouble. The world,
the flesh, and the devil work as a sinister trio to drain our
energies and kill our souls.

"Peace Peace"

When we seek escape from spiritual trouble by denying it exists, we become like the false prophets of Israel.
God says of them, "They have healed the wound of my
people lightly, saying, 'Peace, peace,' when there is no
peace" (Jeremiah 6:14).

The rationale of escape by denial seems simple enough.
If I ignore a problem long enough, like a self-righting ship,
maybe my problem will solve itself. For a denial of the

troubles we face—whether conflict, temptation, suffering, disappointment, regret, misplaced hope, or even our own willful sin—simultaneously means a denial of the magnificent provisions of God's love and care for us. The unexpected and unintended consequence of peace-faking is that we pull a curtain on the God who comforts and rescues. In the imaginary utopia of denial, we do not draw near to God. We do not feel the need of him or his grace. We do not cry out for help and hope. We do not adore him for his covenant love. We miss the feeling of his fatherly hand or the warm glow of his merciful embrace.

But God Is Here

People who belong to God's family in Christ need not deny the reality of spiritual trouble. By God's grace, we can embrace reality. Jesus did not teach his disciples to fake peace. "I have said these things to you, that in me you may have peace. In the world you will have tribulation. But take heart; I have overcome the world" (John 16:33). He spoke plainly to them about the hardships and challenges that come through this fallen world. He offered them, and he offers us, real peace within these troubles. Jesus does not treat us like the psychic physician who merely pretends to help. Jesus offers real peace, not as the world gives, but as only he can give.

Author Dane Ortlund writes, "If you are in Christ, you have a Friend who, in your sorrow, will never lob down a pep talk from heaven. He cannot bear to hold himself at a distance. Nothing can hold him back. His heart is too bound up with yours."[7] Knowing that Jesus is with us in every circumstance, we can leave behind the escape artistry of denial and move forward on the better path of endurance through dependence. Because Jesus overcame sin in all its dimensions—world, flesh, and devil—we can move forward with God's help.

HOW DANA CHANGED

Did Dana grow to engage life's struggles, instead of deny them? He did. He turned to God in prayer, the Spirit grew his faith and hope, and that powered him out of denial and into constructive actions.

Dana's Prayers

By grace, God brought Dana to the point of realizing just how serious his problem with denial was. Through the help of a friend, Dana saw how he was missing key opportunities to serve God and his family by not facing his trouble head-on. In so doing, Dana avoided not only the problems at work and the potential hardships at home but also the beautiful ministry to his family, which God promises to nurture and bless through depending on him in the midst of difficulty.

Dana and his friend began to pray together with a humble sense of his need for God's help. Dana found joy, hope, and courage by agreeing with God that a change was needed. A significant, prayerful turn of heart and mind brought Dana's focus to his first love—God—and onto wise service at work and home. Turning to God and asking for help positioned Dana to reconsider his most entrenched beliefs about life pressures and see how exchanging denial for courageous dependence could make all the difference.

Dana's Belief

In truth, Dana needed a fundamental change of belief. Dana long believed his home should always function as a respite from the cares of his work life. When work became overwhelming, Dana believed his troubles would solve themselves if he imagined they weren't there. So not only did problems at work fester and grow, but his home life deteriorated due to neglect of important challenges and opportunities there.

God replaced his untrue beliefs with the truth about God, work, and home. Most importantly, Dana came to believe the pressures of his office are not mistakes to be ignored but opportunities where God was visiting him with grace. These challenges were what God was using to mold and shape Dana. The transformation of his beliefs enabled Dana to see how God's power is made perfect in weakness (2 Corinthians 12:9). Instead of denying the overwhelming pressure in his life, Dana could rely on God to give him strength and wisdom to endure the challenges he faced at work and at home.

Dana's Action

Dana's change of heart opened the door to experience real solutions in his workplace. He asked his immediate boss for feedback and was able to implement some of the suggestions. He began taking a sincere interest in his coworkers, wishing to minister to them and benefit from their help. When faced with a challenge, Dana became more willing to ask for help or advice, rather than acting as if all was fine or handling trouble in his own, isolated way.

Dana's outlook on work and family life transformed from one of self-focus to a focus on God's pleasure in service to his closest neighbors. Dana started setting his alarm for early in the morning, to spend time with God in Scripture and to pray about his life and work. He prepared his heart for what lay ahead, the pressures as well as the pleasures God planned for his good. When conflicts arose at home, as they inevitably do for all of us, Dana didn't ignore the issue but engaged his wife and kids in helpful ways. Instead of denying the trouble, conflicts became an occasion for growing together as a family. Dana even began asking his wife to share her concerns because he was no longer averse to addressing problems. Instead, he welcomed these honest moments as occasions for ministry to his closest neighbors—his family.

Do you see your reflection in Dana's story? Can you see a little better the nuances of your own inner escape artist? Like Dana, you too can change. Take time now to consider the ways you've sought escape through denial.

WHAT TO PRAY WITH SINCERE HUMILITY

Pray with a focus on God's ultimate control of everything. Ask him to give you a renewed sense of his loving care over your life, even over the whelming flood of trouble you may be facing. You can face these troubles with him because he has the power to face them with you. Pray for eyes to see and a heart to believe that this is true.

Sample Prayer: *God, you are the King of heaven. All things are in your control, and you love me. Please clear my vision to see how you give me the ability to face these trials with you. My life feels overwhelming, but I know you are not overwhelmed. Because you are not wringing your hands in heaven, I can trust you on earth.*

WHAT TO BELIEVE WITH GOSPEL HOPE

Fix your mind on just one primary truth that applies to your life in the difficult moment. Trust a specific promise, like one of the promises above. In the moment of trial, choose to believe God is working in your trial for his glory and your good. Even if you can't see it clearly in the moment, grab on to a specific truth or promise, and hold on tight.

Sample Belief: The gospel of Jesus gives us hope because it announces to us God's ever-present, living hope even in times of trouble. Call to mind a passage we considered earlier in John 16: "I have said these things to you, that in me you may have peace. In the world you will have tribulation. But take heart; I have overcome the world" (v. 33). We can know that God's plan is always to give his people peace as we walk through tribulation (difficulties). Jesus has overcome the world. And because he has overcome the world, we can depend on him. Meditate on this truth, and others like it, throughout difficult days.

HOW TO ACT WITH COURAGEOUS DEPENDENCE

We know that denial of our troubles won't help us. Instead, it will keep us from experiencing the blessings that can come out of trials and prevent us from acting in God-honoring ways. God calls us to trust-filled action. First, pull the problem or situation out from under the rug and look directly at it. Simply stopping to consider the matter carefully can fuel our motivation to deal with it in God-honoring ways. Second, ask wise Christian friends to help you discern the need of the moment. Ask together, "What is at the heart of this problem?" Open the Bible together, looking for similar situations or problems and learn from how God's people addressed them. Third, once you have a sense of what's needed, take the action that seems to most glorify God.

Sample Action: When problems and failures arise, rather than deny their existence, you can acknowledge them. You have a God who lives to help you. If you're facing a conflict with someone else, or if you're feeling weak under the pressures of life, you can embrace the reality of these hardships knowing that God is with you. God in Christ has loved you in spite of who you are, and you have the glorious privilege to act like it!

QUESTIONS FOR REFLECTION

1. Have you faked peace in order to sidestep conflicts or challenges in life? If so, how?

2. What times of trouble tempt you most to deny or downplay the difficulties you face? Are there specific areas of life where denial is a more common response?

3. Having read the insights of Jonathan Edwards, can you see the value of trials more clearly? Which truth do you need to more carefully consider in daily life?

4. What part of Dana's story most resonates with you? In what ways are you, like Dana, most in need of change?

PERSONAL APPLICATION

Make a list of the beliefs that drive you to ignore or minimize the challenges you face. Bring those beliefs to God and identify how they need to change. What Bible passages can you remember that will help you know Jesus better in the midst of your struggle? Then take the very next opportunity you have to obey God by trusting him to help you endure wisely, rather than escape through denial. By grace, you don't have to live in denial anymore.

Chapter 5

WHAT'S WRONG WITH A LITTLE DISTRACTION?

That which is bitter to endure may be sweet to remember.

— Thomas Fuller

When troubles mount do you deal with them by trying to distract yourself? You might be given to distractions if

- when faced with a difficult task, you prioritize less important activities;
- you regularly spend time indulging in excessive media and entertainment;
- your to-do list displays a string of half-finished projects and tasks; or
- difficult times in your life are dealt with by doing something too much—eating, drinking, shopping, gaming, sports, exercise, TV watching, and so on.

DEATH BY DISTRACTION

Taiwanese gamers thought Hsieh was asleep. Then an employee of the urban internet café realized he wasn't sleeping—he lay dead, slumped in the chair where he had sat for three consecutive days. At the time of his death, Hsieh had binged on combat video games for more than seventy-two hours straight. The autopsy confirmed the

thirty-two-year-old man died of sudden death from pro-
longed computer gaming. Hsieh's death followed on the
heels of another death. Another middle-aged man died
following five days of straight video gaming. In both
cases, police were shocked by the complete disinterest
shown by other café patrons, who remained transfixed
by the hypnotic, blue glow of their own screens.[1] While
most of us have never indulged in only pursuing entertainment for three (let alone five) straight days, none of us
are immune to the allure of distraction.

Netflix. Hulu. Disney+. Playstation. Xbox. Nintendo
Switch. Facebook. Instagram. Twitter. Pinterest. The list
could quite possibly grow forever. Like a global cruise
ship, we live in a world bursting with amenities. While
none of these activities are wrong in and of themselves,
each holds the power of potential escape via distraction.

A Subtle Smithing

John Calvin identified our human hearts as "a perpet-
ual forge of idols," or put another way, *the human heart is
an idol factory.*[2] We seldom think about our hearts as idol
factories. After all, we aren't daily kneeling before home-
made altars, offering fruit and burning incense at the feet
of a graven image. Our idol smithing occurs subtly. The
thought of setting up a handmade idol in the place of our
God mortifies us. And yet, Calvin's diagnosis bears out as
we all practice more covert types of idolatry.

For many of us, our idolatry takes center stage when
we turn to a myriad of distractions and discredit God's
power and purposes. As we've seen, every escape route
begins with a false belief or promise. I often find in my

heart the belief that some distracting activity is surely better or more enjoyable than facing trouble with God. When troubles mount or life doesn't seem to be going as we hoped or planned, it's easy to think that God has forgotten us and we are on our own. If that is true, then trying to live from one distraction to the next makes sense. But it isn't true! The truth is that the Lord is always with us. He is always holding us fast (Psalm 139:10). And instead of helping me get through my day, distractions keep me from seeing the promised blessing God has infused in my troubles.

The lure of distraction not only diverts our eyes from the real challenges laid out before us, but distraction also diverts our eyes from the Lord who holds our lives in his hand. When we prefer distraction over dependence, our assurance of God's power and presence shrinks into the periphery of our vision. We lose sight of God's marvelous plans to care for us, change us, satisfy us, and draw us close to himself through the difficult scenarios of life we desperately try to escape. Instead we turn to other things that seem, in our estimation, better able to provide us what we desire or think we need.

Throughout the Bible, we hear the resounding plea to behold our God, to keep our eyes on him, no matter what worldly power threatens to distract. In every overwhelming moment of life, God says, "Watch me, look at me, focus on me, stay with me. I am with you!" Like us, the first disciples were bombarded by pressures, temptations, troubles, doubts, fears, sufferings, and disappointments. Through it all, Jesus continually refocused their eyes on himself. Despite the life of suffering they lived, Jesus promised them a better life, a real and abundant life.

In his book *Your God Is Too Small*, J. B. Phillips says of Jesus, "So far from encouraging them to escape life He came to bring, in His own words, 'life more abundant,' and in the end He left His followers to carry out a task that might have daunted the stoutest heart. Original Christianity had certainly no taint of escapism."[3] Catch those four striking words: *no taint of escapism*. What could have changed? Has a love for distractions captured our hearts? We struggle to maintain a firm grasp on the God who supports us through the overwhelming flood.[4]

THE STORY OF ALYSSA "THE DISTRACTER"

At only twenty-three years old, Alyssa's life is complicated. Eight years ago, Alyssa found herself in a rough place. Poor decisions and unchecked desires led her into drug abuse and sleeping on the streets. One night Alyssa butted heads with a volunteer at a shelter where she often received free food. A scuffle ensued, and Alyssa was arrested. Charged with assault and drug possession, she was held in a minor security women's jail for eight long months.

Alyssa emerged from jail sober but confused and aimless. Her time away brought sobriety but did not kill her gnawing hunger for the euphoric relief provided by her past addiction. She returned to the turbulent dynamics of her mother's home. She knew she couldn't escape from conflict at home by numbing her senses as she had in the past. What else could she do but seek a double escape, from both her contentious relationships and the dangerous allure of her old, self-medicated ways?

She poured herself into several endeavors. She joined online support groups, got a part-time job as a short-order cook, took on a side-hustle, and started a travel blog to record her adventures. Each of these activities could be a positive investment in life and the world, but for Alyssa, they served not as investments but distractions. She packed her life with activities to dodge the real needs within her own heart. By filling every moment of her time, Alyssa didn't have to face the problems of her home and heart. At the end of each day, Alyssa assured herself and others that she was thriving, but in reality, she was avoiding her true troubles by staying busy. Every day, instead of feeling a sense of accomplishment, Alyssa felt more and more anxious. All her activities had not brought peace to her. How could Alyssa replace her practice of distraction with a renewed sense of dependence on God?

FACES OF DISTRACTION

For many of us, difficult days spike our interest in getting away from it all. In the 1970s, a popular soap commercial captured the natural inclination of our hearts. A busy mother runs around the house, answering the ringing phone, corralling screaming children, all while cleaning up the family dog's mess on the floor. She turns to the camera, throws up her hands, and gives an exasperated cry to the heavens: "Calgon, take me away!" The camera cuts away to a full tub as the haggard mom escapes to the comfort of a soothing Calgon bubble bath. The vision resonated with everyone—men and women—who has slumped beneath the oppressive power of a bad day. While there's nothing wrong with relaxing in a tub of warm bubbles, the Calgon commercials tapped into the natural tendency of many hearts, mine included.

When faced with trouble or even just boredom, I often find ways to distract myself. I'm not always a victim of distractions; sometimes I seek them. You too? As masters of diversion, we have a knack for finding ways to distract ourselves from the painful realities of life. Like a factory, we have the ability to churn out distractions whenever we wish. In fact, any of God's good gifts can be leveraged. I'm a master at choosing to do a good thing to avoid a difficult better thing. We could never make an exhaustive list, but it's to our benefit to consider even only two kinds of common distractions.

Buzzing Busyness

Corrie ten Boom, along with her father and sister, helped Jews escape from Nazi persecution during the Holocaust of World War II. Among many nuggets of wisdom, Corrie ten Boom said, "If the devil can't make you sin, he'll make you busy."[5] While the devil cannot make a person do anything, we should heed her wise warning. We find here another example of good things becoming bad things when they take over our lives. Even busyness in the name of church ministry or loving, neighborly deeds can pull us away from more important things or from other God-given responsibilities that we should not neglect.

Perhaps no better example of the distracting power of busyness exists than the account of Martha and Mary. During a long day of travel and ministry, Jesus came to a village called Bethany, where he stopped at the home of Martha and Mary. The account draws a sharp distinction between the two sisters, as Mary sits at the feet of

Jesus and Martha busies herself with hospitable tasks. All of these acts serve noble purposes, and yet they each can sour if allowed to become ultimate in our hearts and minds. In the hustle of well-intentioned ministry to Jesus (the ultimate house guest, mind you), Martha morphs from the hostess with the mostest into a frantic mess. In fact, Martha is so frazzled that the worshiped guest, himself, points out to Martha, "You are anxious and troubled about many things" (Luke 10:41). I imagine those words rang in Martha's ears. Busyness distracted Martha from the most important ministry: sitting at the feet of Jesus.[6]

As I read the account of Martha's busyness, I wonder to myself, *Was Martha escaping by plunging herself in busy work?* The King of the universe, in whom are hidden all treasure and wisdom, sits in her living room. Martha buzzes around like a busy bee. She could be sitting with him listening to words of life. But Martha chooses to occupy herself with other, seemingly important things. This sounds all too familiar to me. I, like Martha, have a tendency to overload my life with busyness and miss out on the most important aspects of knowing Christ. Every time I read this passage, the words of a mentor come to mind. Max Appel, a giant of the faith in my life, repeated to me this advice: "We need to slow down, slow down, slow down, and spend time at the feet of the Master."

Are you like me? When you feel overwhelmed by one part of life, do you immerse yourself in another part of life? There is hope for distracted and distractible people like us. Jesus is ready to receive us, ready to give us grace for today, ready to give us endurance in exchange for escape.

Numbing of Spiritual Senses

When busyness fails to distract our troubled minds, some resort to dulling their physical and spiritual senses as an avenue of escape. The heart and mind (and body) are typically numbed through the application of something that gives us a sense of pleasure and helps us avoid thinking about our troubles.

Abuse of substances like drugs and alcohol is one of the most recognizable forms of sense-numbing distraction. From an early age, parents, teachers, and counselors warn students of the dangers of alcohol and drugs. My early school memories include after-school commercials featuring kid-friendly celebrities urging my friends and me to "just say no to drugs and alcohol." I will never forget the sizzling image of a frying egg as a metaphor of my brain on drugs. God certainly used these campaigns, among other means, to hold me back. And yet, left to my own devices, I still found many other ways to numb myself. Have you?

If escape lures you to abuse substances, I want you to know there's biblical hope and help for you. I encourage you to seek help from reputable, Christian resources and counseling. Books like *Addiction: A Banquet in the Grave* by Ed Welch, as well as gospel-centered addiction counseling are invaluable resources I hope you will seek out (also see www.ccef.org). These addictions not only affect our bodies but our souls as well. So we need careful and wise help to address them.

But other, less lethal numbing distractions abound. Sometimes we look to comforting foods as a means of distraction and escape. Movies, books, travel, scrolling social media, and even smartphone games open a door of immersion in another world. We enter into a fictional story line where the troubles are not our own. Again, there is nothing wrong with enjoying good food or losing oneself in a gripping story. But when hardships hit and life pressures rise, the escape artist within begins searching for diversion. Have you fallen for the distracting allure of numbness? Are you seeking distraction through entertainment or other substances in an effort to push your own life into the background?

Are you numbing the feelings of trial and trouble, instead of pursuing real relief through the endurance Jesus offers? His way surpasses all others, as we learn even more to rest on his sufficient grace.

HOW ALYSSA CHANGED

Remember Alyssa? Coming out of a rocky season of life, she struggled to fight the temptation to distract herself from the real issues of life. The habit of pouring herself into good activities left her with a sense of accomplishment and growth, but problems she sought to escape festered in the background. Eventually she noticed that even though she had given up her drug use and the chaos that caused, she was still restless and anxious.

Alyssa's Prayers

Alyssa's counselor encouraged her to keep a prayer journal where she could write out her thoughts and needs along with a psalm. Her counselor suggested that she turn Psalm 131 into her daily prayer:

O Lord, my heart is not lifted up;
my eyes are not raised too high;

I do not occupy myself with things
   too great and too marvelous for me.
But I have calmed and quieted my soul,
   like a weaned child with its mother;
   like a weaned child is my soul within me.
O Israel, hope in the LORD
   from this time forth and forevermore.

By bringing her concerns to God in childlike humility, she transferred her energies from finding distractions to learning new ways to depend on God. The Holy Spirit strengthened Alyssa to refocus her heart on Christ and his perfect, empowering grace. Specifically, she prayed for wisdom in counting her days. And she prayed for God to grant her discipline to use her time in biblical and constructive ways. So much of her life in the past and in the present was marked by chaos. But through intentional prayer, Alyssa submitted her life to God's faithful orchestration of her life moving forward. And this led to a significant change in the beliefs that directed Alyssa.

Alyssa's Belief

Throughout much of Alyssa's Christian life, she believed that God was present but unable or unwilling to address the family conflicts and the desires for love that had pained her for many years. She believed it was up to her to handle all the difficulties in her life. She had missed out on the gospel blessings of Jesus's good news. In the gospel, God promises grace for resolving conflicts (not just grace for entering heaven). Alyssa had become a casualty of the "gospel gap," which Paul Tripp and Tim Lane identify in their book *How People Change*.[7] What they call the "gospel gap" is simply the space between what we say we believe about God and how we live. In Alyssa's life she said she believed that God was with her, but her actions showed that she really thought life was all up to her.

Alyssa is struggling with *the already* and *the not yet* of the Christian life. While our salvation is secured, we have not yet arrived as the fully sanctified, glorified beings we will one day become. Life is full of trouble, and it's easy to try to escape trouble by filling our lives with substitutes and distractions, as did Alyssa. But as she learned to take all of her troubles to God in prayer, she grew in her faith that he was *really* with her. She studied the Gospel of John and prayed through Jesus's teaching that he is the Vine and we are the branches and we only bear fruit in him (John 15:1–11). Meditating on being united with Christ through the Holy Spirit meant that Alyssa could learn how to live for the glory of God. It was a long process, but she was able to take steps to face the hard family dynamics at home, put to death the addictive desires in her heart, and endure trials and temptations even when she wanted to run. Instead of believing her challenges were problems to avoid or control, Alyssa began believing in God's plan to use them for her good.

Alyssa's Action

With the knowledge that God is working even the hardest experiences of her life for her good, Alyssa began to take hope-filled action. Instead of turning away from conflict, Alyssa enlisted her counselor, her pastor, and a few trusted friends and pastors to help her navigate family relationships. They gave her the support of godly counsel, helping her identify the troubling beliefs and desires of her heart and the great and precious promises found in Scripture. She was also able to talk through the wisest way to be around her family, which helped her sort out when she should move toward her family and when she should pull back. Everyone needs this kind of intentional, Christian help. Do you have friends or pastors who could help you? Reach out to them, the way Alyssa did.

Alyssa's story may sound simple. *Pray, believe, act*, and all is well. It is simple (the gospel always is!), but change does not come quickly and without ongoing effort. In fact, the life of godward trust requires its own kind of persistent dedication, to continue moving forward in faithful allegiance to Christ. For you, me, and Alyssa, moving forward in biblical ways requires a continued watching out for our old ways to return.

WHAT TO PRAY WITH SINCERE HUMILITY

When distractions lure your mind away from difficult realities, try to refocus. God can help you refocus your heart and mind on what he declares most important. Ask God to give you spiritual focus to move forward with his help. Then bring your requests to God, praying specifically about the issues that lay before you. Pray through them one by one, expecting God to clearly answer your prayers.

Sample Prayer: *God, you are in control of everything. The world and everything in it belongs to you. Please, God, help me focus on you in this difficult time. Help me see what needs to change and how you would have me solve these problems. Help me recognize the ways I substitute other things for dependence on you. Help me stop relying on distractions and, instead, to draw close to your loving care.*

WHAT TO BELIEVE WITH GOSPEL HOPE

To battle against destructive distractions, you need a renewed vision for God's work in the present moment. Give focused time to meditation on the good news of Jesus, which can meet you in this current, middle chapter you are living between the beginning and the end of your story. Feed your belief that God's good news is relevant for your life today.

Sample Belief: The good news of Jesus Christ gives grace for today. God is present and working in your life right now, to strengthen you and help you. But in the trouble of life, you lose sight of his ministry to you and see replacements for God as a distraction from your trouble. Instead, Jesus calls us to abide in him. We can rest in this love for us. Jesus is the Vine, and we are the branches. Listen to his words to you and believe them: "Abide in me, and I in you. As the branch cannot bear fruit by itself, unless it abides in the vine, neither can you, unless you abide in me. I am the vine; you are the branches. Whoever abides in me and I in him, he it is that bears much fruit, for apart from me you can do nothing" (John 15:4–5).

HOW TO ACT WITH DEPENDENT COURAGE

When distracting temptations rise, refocus your heart and mind on the trouble at hand. Believing God walks with you, put aside your distraction so you can make forward progress. Humbly enlist other Christians to help you make a plan to honor God by facing the overwhelming issue in your life.

Sample Action: Perhaps you need to ask God for forgiveness because you haven't believed that he is present and can help you and have replaced him with a distraction. Perhaps you need to remove a distracting temptation from your life—disconnect (get rid of?) your gaming system. Remove alcohol from your house. Turn off your TV for a specific period of time. The actions will be different for everyone—the important thing is that you get counsel and help in knowing what you should do, and then help in actually doing it. Reevaluate the focus of your life, so you can move forward through your trouble with God's help. Reach out to a friend, a pastor, or biblical counselor, asking for help to make sense of your trouble. Together you and your helper will be able to evaluate the problem, pray together, and develop a God-honoring plan for change.

QUESTIONS FOR REFLECTION

1. In what ways have you avoided life struggles by pouring your attention into empty or even noble distractions?

2. Which "faces of distraction" show up most often in your daily life?

3. What desires do you see driving you to escape via distraction? What beliefs allow you to pursue these distractions?

4. What changes do you need to make in obedient response to God's offer of help in the gospel? How will you depend on Christ and ask for help from others as you make these changes?

PERSONAL APPLICATION

Take inventory of the time you spend with God, resolving the difficult issues from which you often seek escape. Where do you see time that can be redeemed and used to address the challenges of life, rather than escape them?

Chapter 6

WHAT GOOD COMES FROM DEFLECTING AND DESTROYING?

Left to yourself you would have forsaken these means
of sustaining grace long ago, but the Holy Spirit preserves you
by granting to you the grace to persevere in them.
— Donald Whitney

When you are under pressure, do you try to escape through blaming others and attacking those who are trying to help? You might seek escape through deflection and destruction if

- you push away people who offer to help you;
- in anger you're prone to attacking people not problems;
- you cast yourself in a better light by routinely tearing down or criticizing others;
- isolation or silence brings you more comfort than working out solutions with friends; or
- your troubles and problems all seem to be the fault of others.

THE PATH OF DEFLECT AND DESTROY

When it comes to escaping troubles, one path people often take is blaming others and running from difficult situations. They burn bridges, destroying relationships and lives in the process. I'm thinking of the criticized worker who quits the company with a storm of profanity, leaving bridges burning behind and losing key benefits to care for himself and his family. Or maybe you've heard an unloving spouse shout blame at everyone else, damaging important relationships. Or think of the offended church member who angrily cuts off concerned friends, slipping away from the care of the church.

When life overwhelms, growing anxieties often lead us into a destructive panic. Have you ever felt irritable or angry when squeezed by pressures in life? If left unguarded, you may notice those anxieties can boil over, burning other people. When we feel cornered by life, our hearts tend to lurch out in destructive ways and words. Deflecting and destroying becomes a way to escape pain and trouble without actually resolving it or finding true comfort. When we use these methods of escape, we set ourselves up to repeat the same escape strategies again and again. I have often blamed others for my own failures, so I can escape my own sense of guilt and responsibility. Other times, I've vented my anger with the hope that it will alleviate my hurt feelings or disappointments, which often grow in me when troubles swell and swirl.

But we have good news because Christians are uniquely freed to joyfully lay down our destructive ways, rather than cling to them, for God's glory and the good of others. It's precisely what our King did to redeem us, giving us a better hope of a better kingdom and a better King.

THE DESTRUCTIVE WAY SEEMS RIGHT

This might be the most difficult escapist strategy to combat because it starts with a firm conviction that we are right, while others are wrong and they are to blame for this trouble! But are we so right? What about what God's Word says in Proverbs 16:25? "There is a way which seems right to a man, but its end is the way to death." God thought this was so important that the verse is repeated in Proverbs 14.

This verse emphasizes that we can be deceived. Stop and think for a moment about the jarring end of the verse, "end is the way of death." It's easier to see how being convinced we are right can end in death for others. We look at those who blame others and destroy their lives in the process and we ask:

> How could she do that?
> Why would he say that?
> How does he believe that?

The answer is that way seems right . . . because deceitful sin has dealt its deadly hand, by making the way of death seem right.

The angry, destructive way of dealing with trouble can seem so very right. It reminds us that we must never underestimate the power of sin to blind and persuade and make the deadly ways seem right. Once this happens, the way back becomes steep and difficult. Oh, how sin crouches at the door! With Timothy, we must keep close watch on our life and doctrine (1 Timothy 4:16). God, give us grace. Watch out for us and make us watchful. Give us help and make the way of life seem right. The following story illustrates how trying to escape trouble with deflection and destruction can end a marriage.

A COUPLE DETERMINED TO DEFLECT AND DESTROY

Brenda and Eddie were popular as a couple in high school. Their classmates even voted them prom king and queen. Riding around with the stereo blasting tunes from Eddie's convertible, no other couple was as cute together, and no two people were better company at the local diner. It was assumed Brenda and Eddie would effortlessly live the happily-ever-after life.[1] Fast forward . . .

Over the past fifteen years, Eddie and Brenda lost interest in each other and in their relationship. For Eddie, his rewarding profession consumed much of his time and attention. Reaching the next rung of the corporate ladder held the promise of increased honor and status among his workplace peers. What started as a promising career morphed into a part-time lover, and now Eddie's relationship to Brenda has been replaced by a new wife: work. Brenda is mainly concerned with her children and their lives. When they talk together, it's mainly about the children's activities. Brenda blames Eddie for the distance between them. Eddie blames Brenda. Both have given up on their marriage.

At this point, to destroy their marriage seemed less painful than charting a restorative path forward. They went to a marriage counselor for a brief time, but they used that time to blame each other for their relationship struggles. Each session ended with them feeling cornered on opposite sides of the ring. As time went on, Brenda and Eddie fought harder and harder—against each other.

Sometimes they punished each other with cold shoulders. Other times they fought with searing words of condemnation. In their collective pain and disappointment, lashing out and blowing up and blaming each other seemed the easiest way to escape their problems. Instead of engaging in the hard work of reconciliation, they chose to escape their discomfort and hard feelings by breaking peace. Instead of resolving conflict, they descended into a spiral of anger to create a protective chasm between each other.

Can you relate to Brenda and Eddie? Do you grow restless and frustrated when trouble traps you in a corner? Are your problems always someone else's fault?

Although you may not realize it, we all have much in common with these fellow sinners and sufferers. When we experience the struggles of life—financial, relational, physical—we can all look for someone to blame; we can quickly deflect any responsibility and angrily destroy others. It's so much easier than accepting responsibility, isn't it? But is it? You can escape a marriage, but what happens in a new relationship? If we don't accept that we have responsibility, we will recreate the same struggles again and again.

Perhaps you are someone who breaks relationships, rules, things, or people as a means of escaping the hard circumstances of life. In Christ, we have real hope for change and peace. God, give us grace. Watch out for us and make us watchful. Give us help and make the way of life seem right.

BREAKING PEACE

In chapter 4, I told you a story about Tony Agpaoa, a fraudulent surgeon. He made money off his patients by pretending to heal them. His mode of operation matches a common way we respond to spiritual trouble and conflict. We fake peace.

A troubled marriage has Brenda and Eddie searching for a way of escape. Rather than enduring their troubles, honoring their vows, and drawing close to God, they think of ways to destroy their marriage, even to destroy one another. In a twisted way, destruction promises a relief from the pressures of life. Peace-breaking can take many forms. If someone levels a serious accusation, a peace-breaker might return fire with a stinging rebuke. When a sinful habit brings shame on the family, a peace-breaker might sever ties with his parents. Perhaps the most extreme examples of breaking peace show up on the nightly news and crime report shows. As investigators snoop around, a peace-breaker will snuff out the witnesses of their crime. For a brief time, feelings of peace surge, but in the end their sin finds them out. The unavoidable reality proves, as among peace-fakers, real peace always eludes peace-breakers.[2] Rather, only when we navigate trouble with dependence on God do we know the peace that passes all understanding (Philippians 4:7). Brenda and Eddie (and perhaps you?) are looking for peace by trying to escape. But real peace only comes from a growing love for Jesus.

I AM HERE

South African pastor Andrew Murray was in bed with severe back pain, in the home of someone who hosted him on a preaching trip. The person who attended to him one day in 1895 came to his room. She said a troubled woman had knocked on the door asking for his counsel. He said,

"Just give her this advice I'm writing down for myself; it may be that she'll find it helpful."

The attendant dictated Murray's advice for the troubled woman:

> In time of trouble say, "First, he brought me here. It is by his will I'm in this strait place; in that I will rest." Next, "He will keep me here in his love, and give me grace in this trial to behave as his child." Then say, "He will make the trial a blessing, teaching me lessons he intends me to learn, and working in me the grace he means to bestow." And last, say, "In his good time he can bring me out again. How, and when, he knows."[3]

Four truths emerge and offer us timely help in the moment of heat.

When facing a difficult situation we should profess with confidence, I am here (1) by God's appointment, (2) in his keeping, (3) under his training, and (4) for his time. The only way to work through overwhelming hardships is by remembering God's loving care in all times. When we feel cornered by circumstances we can't control, we can know God holds us and our circumstances in his hands. What do we do next? Instead of blaming others or lashing out, we pray in Jesus's name for his help.

WHAT TO PRAY WITH SINCERE HUMILITY

Feeling the pull of destructive anger and frustration can provide a path to humility, when we come to see our need for grace. Often when we are overwhelmed, grace is the most important request of God. You need grace to cool your frustrations and point you in a more godly direction. Ask God for grace to help in your time of need. In humility you can approach his throne of grace with confidence, asking for him to minister his grace to your heart.

When you are tempted to blame and attack, talk to Jesus and ask him to remind you that he is better! Thank him that he has redeemed you from the pit. You can pray for the help you need in the name of Jesus. Refuse temptation in Jesus's name!

Sample Prayer: *God, my frustrations have risen above my head. Please give me grace for this moment, to cool the heat of my heart and help me look to you as my hope and salvation in times of trouble. I pray in Jesus's name for help from above to resist the temptation to blame and attack. Forgive me and help me!*

WHAT TO BELIEVE WITH GOSPEL HOPE

Who do you believe holds ultimate control in your life? If you believe everything depends on you and your ability, frustrations will rise. You may find yourself in a self-destructive cycle of anger. But the truth remains: everything depends on God. He is the builder who knows what to do and how to do it, and he even has the power to do what's needed in and through you.

Escape promised Brenda a better life if she would simply break her marriage covenant with Eddie. As do we, she needs Christ-centered hope to invade her situation. The loving control of our Good Shepherd doesn't mean our lives will be easy and smooth. But instead his perfect care offers us stability, resolve, and self-control when otherwise we might use ungodly anger to our advantage. We hear this clearly reflected in the words of James, "let every person be quick to hear, slow to speak, slow to anger; for the anger of man does not produce the righteousness of God" (James 1:19–20). Our temptation must be replaced by the biblical truth that honoring God disarms our desire to speak rashly or give in to our own demands. We can patiently walk through trouble because God walks with us in Christ.

Sample Belief: The author of Hebrews reminds us, "For every house is built by someone, but the builder of all things is God" (Hebrews 3:4). Set your heart upon God as the one who works in and through you and who holds ultimate responsibility for your life.

HOW TO ACT WITH DEPENDENT COURAGE

Escapism tempts us to lash out when life overwhelms. This comes from a driving sense that we are in control and must ensure our plans are achieved. We often feel that our own ability to control life and other people will help us escape the heartache or trouble we face. But the person who courageously depends on God acts with the knowledge that God controls the world and that our lives operate in service to him. To act with courageous dependence on God, you must center your life on one question: How can I glorify and enjoy God in this difficult time. Acting out of a desire to magnify God's glory and maximize your gladness in him will keep you back from self-destructive ways.

Sample Action: Ask someone you trust to help you notice when you are blaming others for your struggles and/or when you are attacking others instead of facing a difficult situation. Who do you trust to speak truth to you about these matters? Start to keep a journal and note when you get angry. Ask someone else how they viewed the situation. If you're facing a complicated problem, share it with someone you know who loves God and lives with wisdom and composure. Reach out to this person, a pastor, or biblical counselor, asking for help to make sense of your trouble. Together you and your helper will be able to evaluate the problem and pray together; they can comfort you and help you develop a God-honoring plan for change. And then continue this edifying relationship of accountability, so you will have ongoing help to change in the future and not only in the present moment of crisis.

QUESTIONS FOR REFLECTION

1. In what ways have you attempted to solve problems or gain comfort through destruction, perhaps even self-destruction? Have you broken relationships, objects, or something else?

2. How is peace-breaking similar to peace-faking?

3. List three lessons you can learn from Brenda and Eddie's story. How are you like them? How does their story reflect your need for change?

PERSONAL APPLICATION

The next time you're tempted to escape from a spiritual struggle, call to mind the advice Andrew Murray gave to the troubled woman. Begin regularly meditating, in seasons of difficulty and ease, on Murray's key truths: you are here (1) by God's appointment, (2) in his keeping, (3) under his training, and (4) for his time.

Chapter 7

WHAT HOPE IS THERE IF I
JUST WANT TO DIE?

*Heartache forces us to embrace God out of desperate, urgent
need. God is never closer than when your heart is aching.*

— Joni Eareckson Tada

You might see death as a good way to escape if

- you hope for heaven more as a relief from present trouble than for eternal fellowship with Christ;
- in the midst of trouble, you feel the ultimate pressure to make things better;
- you view death as the easiest or only resolution to difficult circumstances of life, or
- you fantasize about the world being a better place without you.

WELCOMING DEATH

Have you ever wished for death to relieve you of your difficult life or situation? I'd like to say no one responds this way, but I know the truth. In brief moments of hardship—or long seasons of suffering—the desire to escape through death lurks in many of our hearts. I confess that in times of discouragement and dissolution, my heart has contemplated this most ultimate escape. I know I'm not alone.

Perhaps you've felt the dread of despair that makes death seem like the only way out. As a pastor, I've sat with mothers in the agonizing pain of losing a child. In the moment of heartache and loss, laughing and smiling and the joy of life seem like utter impossibilities. In the darkness of depression, we simply can't imagine how the sun will ever shine again. Even the reassuring voices of loving friends can't seem to reach us. Arguments fall flat. Encouragements feel empty. Commands to cheer up are impossible to obey. God seems distant. Under such heartache, the thought of death creeps into even the bravest of us.

The World Health Organization reports nearly three-quarters of a million people die by suicide each year.[1] I believe millions more think about death in troubling times. The thought of death as an escape doesn't always come with a credible threat or plan. And this further shows how our desire for escape comes naturally.

Through counseling and chaplaincy, I've known a number of friends who struggled with these thoughts and others who have carried them out. Like few other things, suicide portrays the deceit, ugliness, hopelessness, and utter pain of sin and despair. The Bible and our experience show the propensity of every fallen heart to consider desperate measures during desperate times. "Why did you bring me out from the womb? Would that I had died before any eye had seen me" (Job 10:18).

Is there a more sinister scheme of sin than the coaxing of our hearts to indulge deadly thoughts? But as we've considered, there is a better way. Rather than seeking escape from life, we can turn to God, who offers us shelter from the storm beneath the shadow of his wings (Psalm 57:1). And we don't take shelter with a sour, angry, grudging

God; instead our refuge is in the love of God who gave us his Son so that we could be close to him forever.

HARMING YOURSELF

Another common struggle tracks along similar lines of suicide. Self-harm promises a kind of escape that is hard to imagine by those who haven't faced it. While the most familiar form of self-harm is cutting, it's not the only way. I've seen counselees who punch themselves, pull hair, scratch to the point of drawing blood, and so on. Because it's easy to hide the evidence of self-harm, becoming trapped in a private self-injury cycle is more common than most people know.

As stress, anger, or frustration with life rises, temptations to self-harm rise as well. Certainly, harming ourselves can rise from a sense of guilt, leading to the intention of punishing ourselves for something we've done. But often the motive is escape. When life feels hopeless, dull, or numbing, inflicting our own pain offers a kind of relief or escape from our consuming troubles. But despite a feeling of momentary relief, in reality self-harm brings more trouble, more guilt, more stress. The cycle of despair continues.

In both temptations of suicide and self-harm, Jesus offers us real hope of change. When we experience guilt, despair, and/or self-hatred, the love of Christ can shine through the darkness. Jesus paid the price for our sins, setting us free from guilt by faith in him. Instead of hating us, Jesus chose to set his everlasting love on us. Through his own death on the cross, he opened a new and living. way for us to look away from ourselves and to set our eyes on him and his wondrous promises.

BIG PROMISES AND PITHY PLATITUDES

In moments of despair—when suicidal thoughts swarm and self-harm promises relief—we do not need platitudes. We need robust, gospel-centered hope and help. We need truth that can uplift our hearts, transform our desires, embolden our beliefs, and give us endurance. We need Christ who endured the cross, despised the shame, died in our place, and rose again for us, so we could live enduringly in him (Hebrews 12:2). I can tell you from personal experience that with Jesus and his Word, there is hope for you. My own family knows well this painful battle.

My wife faced significant struggles for many years. I've asked her to write a letter to you, a fellow struggler who may be in the deep darkness of despair and wishing you could just escape once and for all.

A LETTER TO THE DESPAIRING

My Dear Friend,

I am so thankful for this moment to write a letter to you. I wish I could get to know you in person. When I'm having a hard time, as you may be having now, I love to hear encouragement from friends who love me. In this letter, I simply want to encourage you with my story. In a simple way, maybe I can be a friend to you.

I want you to see the great hope there is in Christ. Whether you face the most serious of problems or something seemingly minor in your life that you think can never change, I hope my story will help you. If you are a believer in Christ, through the power of the Holy Spirit and with the help of God's Word, you can change.

If you're struggling to endure a hard life—wanting to escape—I want you to hear from me that God and his Word alone have the power to help you renew your courage and trust God during these dark times. Maybe my story will give you hope.

I grew up in a Christian family and was taught about God. But in middle school I started becoming increasingly concerned with my appearance. By the time I started high school, I obsessed over my body, and over what people thought about me. I began starving myself and abusing laxatives, and it wasn't long before this way of life consumed me in a spiral of dread.

I cried for hours at night, dreading the next day. I didn't want to wake up. I would stay up for as long as I could because I didn't want to wake up the next morning and realize I'm still me. I was hopeless. Over the next eight years I spent time in six different facilities, on various occasions. Doctors prescribed medications, and even electroconvulsive therapy (ECT). I attended group and individual counseling multiple times a day.

I bounced between begging him to help me, and then venting my anger about the unfairness of my life. *God, you have done this to me! I don't deserve this!* I was self-absorbed. I've realized over the years that I simply cannot be consumed with myself and focused on my God at the same time. I needed a radical change of perspective. But that change was still a long way off. The doctors held out little hope for me. How could I cope with such darkness for seventy-five more years! I did not want to live! But a big change was just around the corner.

I met Rush, my future husband, and for a time the despair lifted, but then it closed in again.

A year after my ECT, Rush and I moved to North Carolina to attend seminary. We had been married for a couple years and did not know yet the potential help which lay ahead in Christ. I met a biblical counselor who spoke about the hope of change that comes by walking with Jesus. The Bible began speaking to the very root issues I struggled with for so long.

I grew more in just one year than I had in the twenty-five years before. When I think back about what made the biggest difference in those days, I can say without hesitation the Word of God worked a profound, sweet, uplifting miracle in me. In many ways, God's Word redirected my gaze from my disappointments and shortfalls to his overwhelming grace and love toward me. With his faithfulness in view, living to glorify him moment by moment became a delight—certainly a complete new experience for me. The burden of living up to his standard was lifted by Christ who gave all for me. The more I understood the gentle and lowly Jesus in the Scriptures, the more my heart brightened with joy in him.

Like we all do, I still struggle from time to time. But I have found a new and living way to endure the hard things in my life. You can too. In Christ and through his Word there is great hope for real, lasting change. My story is one of many that shows the beauty of the gospel, the mercy of Jesus, and the value of God's Word.

As I've studied the Scriptures since then, Psalm 39 has shed a whole new light on all the time I spent looking for answers within myself. I read,

> O LORD, make me know my end
>> and what is the measure of my days;
>> let me know how fleeting I am!
> Behold, you have made my days a few handbreadths,
>> and my lifetime is as nothing before you.
> Surely all mankind stands as a mere breath! . . .
> And now, O Lord, for what do I wait?
>> My hope is in you. (Psalm 39:4–5, 7)

If you're struggling with depression and despair and even thoughts of death, I want you to know there is hope. Please contact a trusted Christian friend or pastor who can help you grow and change and endure, the way they helped me. There is light after the darkness.

Depending on God with you,

Kathryn Witt

HOPE FOR US ALL

If you, like Kathryn, have ever felt despair, depression, or wished for the release of death, I hope you can see the shining hope and help of Christ available even in the darkest of times. You may feel enveloped and consumed by despair. We want you to know by our own testimony that our God reigns even in the darkness. We can rejoice with the psalmist,

> If I say, "Surely the darkness shall cover me,
>> and the light around me be night,"
> even the darkness is not dark to you;
>> the night is as bright as the day,
>> for darkness is as light with you. (Psalm 139:11–12)

By depending on God, by faith in Christ, as a child of his grace, you have every reason to rejoice. But it will take time and help.

If you are struggling with dark thoughts of death, there is help available to you. I encourage you to reach out for help. Seek out a faithful pastor, biblical counselor, or mature Christian friend. Ask them for help. Organizations like the Christian Counseling and Educational Foundation (ccef.org), the Association of Certified Biblical Counselors (biblicalcounseling.com), and others can help you find a competent and caring counselor in your area. Don't wait another minute, for in Christ, light is shining just over the edge of darkness. If you have been contemplating suicide or other forms of self-harm, put down this book and contact a close friend or call your local emergency number (911 in the US, 112 in Europe). Tell this person what you're thinking and ask for help. We all need help; don't hesitate to ask for it. You're not alone.

DEADLY HEART DYNAMICS

The first step in defeating dark thoughts of death is to know our hearts. No matter what hard situation we face, we know our thoughts come from within us. Our most challenging, destructive problems are internal—they are the sins and sorrows that spring from our hearts (Luke 6:45). For this reason God sent his Son into the world on a rescue mission. Under the curse of sin, our world—our hearts—need God's otherworldly grace to come down. But he didn't come merely to change our circumstances. Jesus came down carrying sin-treating solutions for our sin-sick hearts (Titus 2:11–14). He came to change *us*. What an astounding thought! If you're suffering under a dark cloud, I know it's hard to see this. But if you listen closely for the truth, God can shine his light into your heart.

Still, in some dark seasons, we don't believe Jesus can change us. We don't believe there is hope in our current situation. We don't see how God could possibly bring good out the despair we are experiencing. Even when we are reminded of his soul-satisfying power, our hearts may continue to believe that death is the better way to find the relief we long for. When this occurs, one key source of our inner trouble becomes evident: our beliefs. On top of bodily struggles (like thyroid conditions) and the pressures of a fallen world, untrue beliefs can lie at the root of our occasional (or frequent) desire for death. Consider some of the common, untrue beliefs we entertain during times of despair.

- Everyone would be better off without me.
- Death will solve everything.
- If God loved me, he would let me escape my problems.
- God has forgotten me. There's no hope!
- I simply can't do what God expects of me.
- I'm ruining everyone's life being this way.
- Nothing will ever change!

These internal voices of belief speak convincingly, but they are mistaken. In our right minds, we see their flaws. But when trials and troubles overwhelm our hearts, our mindful composure dissolves, and we choose to believe the otherwise unbelievable.

Will everyone really be better off? Will death really solve everything? Am I fit to dictate to God how he should love me? Has God actually forgotten me? Is all hope really gone? Has God really failed to give me what I need to follow him? Am I really powerful enough to "ruin" everyone's life? Do I truly have sufficient reason to believe that nothing will change?

We need the renewal of mind Paul wrote of: "Do not be conformed to this world, but be transformed by the renewal of your mind, that by testing you may discern what is the will of God, what is good and acceptable and perfect" (Romans 12:2). When despair drives us toward escape, a war of beliefs is raging. In those seasons, we need the truth of God to replace our unbiblical thinking with biblical, life-giving truth.

But this work is no easy task. A simplistic plan like "read a verse, say a prayer" will not suffice. We fight fiercely—lives are at stake—not with only one verse of Scripture but the whole counsel of God, not with one prayer for help but prayers unceasing. We cannot fight this daunting battle alone. We need other Christians to support, comfort, and encourage us. We need them to share Scripture with us and pray with and for us. The Spirit will use our spiritual resources united together and empowered by God to replace our despairing beliefs with the truth of God's love.

YOU'RE NOT ALONE

Thoughts of death often bring with them alarm and an even greater sense of despair. *What am I thinking? No one else is struggling like this!*, we may think to ourselves. We feel life is spinning out of control. The centripetal force of these thoughts and feelings fuels the downward spiral of deepening dread. And in these times, a surprising truth has soothed my soul more than others. You might expect solace would come through a friend's well-intentioned promises that "It's all going to be ok in the end" or "You can do it." But even in our despair, we know these promises do not hold water. However, I've found a surprising source of comfort from three simple words in 1 Corinthians 10:13: "common to man."

In a season of depression and despair, when thoughts of death grow, we tend to define ourselves as the special case. But Paul reminds us that "No temptation has overtaken you that is not *common to man*." In his sovereign wisdom, God has ensured that our struggles are common. So there is no need to fear or panic. Our brothers and sisters in Christ are facing (or have faced) similar trials and temptations. We take comfort in knowing that we do not suffer alone but side by side. And our sufferings are not unique to us but common among us. Three key benefits are ours when we embrace this comforting truth.

Three Benefits of Commonality

1. You can know you are not alone in your suffering or in your desire for escape. Do not underestimate the sweet salve of this truth. As you read in her own words, my wife has struggled with the downward pull of depression and despair. During my wife's darker moments, I recall the spiritual pain of her despair. Yes, there was pain from disappointments. There was pain from grief and sadness. But deeper still was the pain of feeling alone. We often buy into the deceptive feeling that we have been deserted by

God, but we also feel abandoned by everyone else because no one else seems to understand. Well, friend, those three inspired words can fill you with a true and abiding comfort because they reveal that your suffering and heartache are not an unknown rarity. You're not strange or alone.

2. Because your suffering is common to man, a common solution is in Christ. Rather than feeling like all hope is lost because the cure to our troubles is as rare as the trouble itself, we find through Scripture that God's solution is equally common: his transforming grace. By grace alone, sufficient resources of help and hope belong to us, and they are not found in a system but in a Person. Three of the most wondrous words in all of Scripture can also be found in 1 Corinthians 10:13: "God is faithful." He is our sovereign, good, and wise King. We can trust him!

3. Because our struggles are common to man, we have hope that the Holy Spirit can help us persevere through them. He has helped so many of our brothers and sisters in Christ who have gone before us. The example of many other people who courageously depended on Christ in the turbulent waters that we currently face can be a source of wisdom and encouragement. Like the deep-sea captain who fears not the crashing waves because others have gone before him, we must try not to fear, knowing many brothers and sisters have gone before us.

In Good Company

In our moments of despair, courage often comes through hearing from others who endured before you. I know this firsthand because of the journey I have traveled with my wife, Kathryn, whose story I briefly told in my book *Diehard Sins*. Her struggle with depression and anxiety took her through suicide attempts, in and out of psych wards, and eventually into biblical counseling (which was a saving grace). Even today, when times are hard, a desire for escape may well up in her heart. Yet, by God's grace, she is not where she used to be.

I'd like to introduce you to a few other suffering yet enduring souls of the past and present. William Cowper, Charles Spurgeon, and Joni Eareckson Tada stand as shining examples to us in times of oppressive temptation and trial. As you continue reading, hear about and from them and be encouraged with me.

William Cowper

A prolific hymn writer, life was filled with struggle and suffering from the earliest days of William Cowper's life. At the age of six, his mother died. His father sent him to boarding school. The rigors and pressures of school led him into life-dominating depression. Continual disappointment and losses culminated in a series of mental breakdowns. Three times Cowper attempted suicide; an asylum became his horrific home. Throughout it all, the Hound of heaven pursued William with his grace.[2]

While under the care of his asylum doctor, Cowper was converted. Even still, his tendency to isolation and escape persisted. But God brought a new friend into his life—fellow hymn writer John Newton,[3] who helped Cowper endure by grace.[4] A new outlook on his troubled past and present settled in on William. In 1773, Cowper wrote his hymn "God Moves in a Mysterious Way," which exhorts us to "Judge not the Lord by feeble sense, / But trust Him for His grace; / Behind a frowning providence / He hides a smiling face." William Cowper learned how to courageously depend on God, even when dark clouds hung low.

Charles Spurgeon

The "Prince of Preachers" holds the admiration of thousands (if not millions) of pastors and Christians worldwide. His courage in the face of opposition, commitment to the Word of God, and genuine love for people combine to form a portrait of excellence. Carl F. H. Henry considered Spurgeon "one of evangelical Christianity's immortals."[5] While this is true, if this is the only picture of Spurgeon you know, then you know only half of the story.

Spurgeon swam in deepest theology, ran in godly circles, and advanced the kingdom of God like few others. And yet, for much of his life, he battled depression, often wrestling with a longing for death.[6] While Cowper saw great loss in his life, Spurgeon saw great loss in his church. One evening at Surrey Hall, where Spurgeon preached, several troublemakers cried "Fire!" igniting panic among the attendees. Seven people died, and many others were seriously injured in the stampede. Compounding his melancholy disposition, the tragedy deeply affected Spurgeon, nearly paralyzing him in life and ministry. Yet through it all, Spurgeon learned the art of endurance by clinging to Jesus. In his book *Morning and Evening*, Spurgeon wrote, "Mark then, Christian, Jesus does not suffer so as to exclude your suffering. He bears a cross, not that you may escape it, but that you may endure it. Christ exempts you from sin, but not from sorrow. Remember that, and expect to suffer."[7] The Prince of Preachers was a prince of enduring grace too!

Joni Eareckson Tada

If you've not heard the story of Joni Eareckson Tada, I encourage you to read about it in her book *When Is It Right to Die?* Joni Eareckson Tada lived an exuberant teenage life in the 1960s. She enjoyed riding horses with friends, hiking, tennis, and swimming. One glorious day near the end of summer, Joni suited up for a swim with friends in the Chesapeake Bay. With youthful vigor, she dove headfirst into the water, just as she had many happy times before. But for this dive, she misjudged the depth, and the angle of her entry into the water caused her head to hit the hard bottom. Under the weight of impact, her neck snapped. Her youthful vigor evaporated in that catastrophic moment. A friend rescued her from the water, and Joni was taken to the hospital.

Her days in the hospital turned into weeks, and weeks in the hospital turned into months. Joni's spinal cord was severed, and she had become paralyzed from the shoulders down. Since 1967, Joni Eareckson Tada has lived her life in a wheelchair without use of her legs and limited use of her hands. Most of us can only imagine the agony of waking up as a mobile teenager in the morning and going to sleep paralyzed that night. Suddenly, all of her dreams were gone. Joni's tragic loss plunged her into the depths of despair where escape seemed the only option.

While lying in a hospital bed soaked with midnight tears, Joni begged for death to take her away. When left alone, she poured what strength she had into thrashing her head back and forth, hoping she might break her neck at a higher point. She wanted the nightmare to end. But the Lord, who is with us in our suffering, did not allow Joni to succeed. He had other plans. Through her suffering, Joni learned and now teaches a monumental truth: "Heartache forces us to embrace God out of desperate, urgent need. God is never closer than when your heart is aching."[8]

The decades that followed the accident brought Joni marvelous blessings in life, love, and ministry. Only in eternity will we know how many people have been comforted, converted, and blessed by the grace of God through her.

Along with Cowper and Spurgeon and countless others, Joni's story is one of courageous dependence. By learning to depend on God and his good care, Joni can sympathetically exhort you to look up when despair is growing and all you want is an escape. "Your life is not a boring stretch of highway. It's a straight line to heaven. Look at the fields ripening along the way. Look at the tenacity and endurance. Look at the grains of righteousness. You'll have quite a crop to harvest . . . so don't give up!"[9] Joni spoke these words of encouragement because she first learned their truth through thousands of days in pain, in weakness, in need of assistance.

Throughout the past twenty-five years of pastoral ministry, I've known scores of Christians who have struggled in these serious ways yet come to know the precious comforts of Christ. The struggles of depression are so common, as well as the experiences of God's grace at work, that I have no doubt you know people in your church or wider Christian circle who would gladly walk with you.

I encourage you to reach out to a pastor or trusted friend who can help you or connect you with someone who can.

WHAT TO PRAY WITH SINCERE HUMILITY

When dark clouds of heartache and despair roll in, praying our need with humility cannot be underestimated. In fact, these prayers have such value that the Holy Spirit will pray for us when words fail. When you pray in the dark, ask God to comfort and sustain, give light and grace. Pray he would appear ever clearer and closer than you've known him to be. True humility in prayer acknowledges your great need for God. Ask him to be your hope of all hopes in this dark time.

Sample Prayer: *God, you are my hope and help. I'm struggling to see you, but by your Word I know you're with me. Grant me eyes to see your faithfulness and love, and give me a heart to depend upon you in this hard time.*

WHAT TO BELIEVE WITH GOSPEL HOPE

The best beliefs are gospel beliefs, which preach from within our hearts the surpassing value and power of God's good news. What more could we ask in times of death and darkness than for good news to brighten and sustain our hearts? So when life overwhelms, we need constant reminders of God's great love shown to us in Christ. The more we settle our hearts on him, the more strength we have when life overwhelms.

Sample Belief: Because dark times tend to tire us so much, it's helpful to cling to one big promise at a time. Even a short verse of Scripture can pack a powerful reminder of God's faithfulness and the hope we have in Christ. Focus your mind and hope on the precious promises of God, which remain certain when life feels like too much:

> You keep him in perfect peace
>   whose mind is stayed on you,
>   because he trusts in you.
> Trust in the Lord forever,
>   for the Lord God is an everlasting rock. (Isaiah 26:3–4)

HOW TO ACT WITH DEPENDENT COURAGE

As a person committed to humble dependence on God, you can focus your life and action on knowing and pleasing God in the present moment. Every Christian lives within the liberating reality that our circumstances do not dictate how we must feel, think, or live. The hard situations we face in life may influence or tempt us, but they need not control us. This reality provides the key to depending on God and pushing back against the world, the flesh, and the devil. Keeping in mind this reality will open up a door for courageous action with God's help.

Sample Action: Is life tempting you to give up on yourself, God, and others? Take hold of the liberating reality that you can act against that temptation. Instead of giving in to despair, nurture hope with another Christian who loves you and will walk with you. Rather than isolating from others, engage people with love.

QUESTIONS FOR REFLECTION

1. Have you ever wished for death to relieve you of your difficult life or situation?

2. What ungodly beliefs do you find at work in your heart during your darkest thoughts of escape?

3. What did you think about Kathryn's realization that not only did she need to eliminate the untrue beliefs and ruling desires, but she also needed to see them replaced with new and better ones? Is there a belief, thought, or action that you've tried and failed to get rid of in the past? Is there a better belief, thought, or action that you could try replacing it with?

4. How has God met you in your heartache and despair with comfort, hope, and help? If you can't identify a time when you have had this experience, pray that you will experience God's nearness today, and talk with a trusted Christian friend or pastor about this.

PERSONAL APPLICATION

At the end of each day, take ten minutes to review the struggles you faced and how you responded. Note the times and ways when a courageous dependence on God fades, as the difficult darkness of despair begins to rise. How can you look to Christ and other helpful Christians for aid and comfort? This kind of regular review will help you see where attention is needed in your daily life.

Chapter 8

THERE'S LIGHT AFTER DARKNESS

Faith-healing is grand, but faith-enduring is grander.

— Charles Spurgeon

If the Christian life had a motto, what would it be? A survey of suggestions would return a host of answers—some good, some bad, and some downright illogical. Despite the impossibility of narrowing them down to a single, all-encapsulating motto for the Christian life, one motto stands out in my mind: *post tenebras lux*.

A SUFFERABLE ERA

As we survey the course of biblical history, the unique Latin phrase *post tenebras lux* expresses the profound, central experience of knowing God. *Post tenebras lux* means "after darkness light." Look at almost any era of God's people, and you will find this simple motto stamped in deep red ink. After the darkness of their fall into sin, the light of the first gospel promise shined on Adam and Eve. After the darkness of wandering in the wilderness, the light of the Promised Land dawned on Israel. After the darkness of four hundred years of silence to close the Old Testament, Jesus, the Light of the World, broke out in the New Testament. After the darkness of persecuting the church by Paul's unbelief, the light of Christ invaded the heart of the apostle. *Post tenebras lux* marks every page in the Bible, but it doesn't end there. The powerful light of God has continued to scatter darkness in every era since.

In Christ, we have the hope of *post tenebras lux*: after darkness light. By holding tight to this confession of our faith, we, too, can know God's gracious gift of endurance. We must remember—as did the enduring saints of old—that our hope and joy rests in God, who is faithful and will provide us a way to escape sin and endure hardship for his glory.

SEEN vs. UNSEEN

When faithful Christians are able to endure hardships, it's because they know that, because of Jesus, God loves them, and even when they might not see it, he is at work in their present struggles. From beginning to end, the Scriptures draw a distinction between two realities: seen and unseen. We live every moment of life between these two realities. However, the appeal to escape often results from a failure to live by the unseen reality, where God works in marvelous ways. In fact, as I consider my own propensity to run from hardship, I realize how often I fail to appreciate or even consider God's loving care at work behind the scenes. As a result of his love, our hope of endurance will grow. A couple of examples can help us tighten our grip on the distinction between the seen and unseen realities of life.

First, an example from the Old Testament appears in the book of Psalms. Reflecting on difficult seasons of life, King David wrote, "For my father and my mother have forsaken me, but the LORD will take me in" (Psalm 27:10). A single verse expresses both realities. In the seen reality, David said those who should love him most had forsaken him. What a difficult and disappointing experience! Anytime those closest to us turn their backs, we are prone to despair and lose hope. But David did not lose hope. Instead, he squared his attention to the ultimate reality of God's care in the unseen: "but the LORD will take me in." David didn't deny or distract himself from the reality of painful abandonment. He didn't lash out in destruction or sink into inconsolable gloom. Instead, David expressed his heartache to the God who cares. When all else failed him, God did not. God pulled him close, satisfied his soul, and walked with him through the dark valley of desertion. The unseen reality overshadowed the seen reality.

Second, a similar example from the New Testament appears in the life of Jesus. Jesus assured his disciples, "Behold, the hour is coming, indeed it has come, when you will be scattered, each to his own home, and will leave me alone. Yet I am not alone, for the Father is with me" (John 16:32). Jesus foretold trouble on the horizon. In the hour of need, his disciples scattered, leaving him to face a dark hour alone. When the heat turned up, his friends turned out. In this difficult moment, Jesus showed us the better way. He infused the present moment with truth from the unseen. Though his disciples left him alone in the seen reality, he was not alone in the unseen reality. His Father, whom he perfectly depended upon, remained close to him. Again, the unseen reality overshadowed the seen reality.

We have in Christ the immense joy of living by the unseen reality. Just as Jesus lay at peace in the hull of the boat, while the waves and winds swirled about his frantic disciples, we, too, have spiritual resources available to us that can enable us to calmly endure trouble. The apostle

Paul wrote, "We do not lose heart. Though our outer self is wasting away, our inner self is being renewed day by day. For this light momentary affliction is preparing for us an eternal weight of glory beyond all comparison, as we look not to the things that are seen but to the things that are unseen. For the things that are seen are transient, but the things that are unseen are eternal" (2 Corinthians 4:16–18). In all kinds of trials and tribulations, Paul displayed in himself and instilled in others a courageous dependence upon God.

Even as I type these words, a global pandemic swirls around the globe, riots break out in the streets, and only uncertainty seems certain. We have good reasons to fret and fear and escape. But we have many more and better reasons to depend wholly on God's grace. He can be trusted implicitly because he is explicitly supreme in love and truth. He causes light to shine after, in, and through darkness!

HOLDING FAST TO OUR FAITHFUL FATHER

We have many reasons to endure, but the faithfulness of God shines as the ultimate reason. The question of God's love has been answered. He proved his faithful love for his people on the cross of Jesus. Do you remember seeing this earlier in the simple words of 1 Corinthians 10:13? Exhorting believers toward endurance through temptation and trial, Paul grounded his readers' endurance in the fact that "God is faithful."

The same rationale appears throughout Hebrews as well. On every page, Jesus is shown to be better than everything and everyone else. In a world of counterfeit hopes and promises, Jesus shines forth as better than Moses, better than the high priests of Israel, better than the old covenant sacrifices, better than the angels, better than ease and comfort, better than worldly wishes and dreams. Jesus is the better Prophet, the better Priest, the better King. Because he is better, we hold fast to him. Sent to us by our faithful Father, Jesus our Redeemer helps us in every way. He has been tried and tempted, pressed and pressured, maligned and mistreated, grieved and full of sorrow in this life. Yet he stands out as the hope of our joy and glory—One who has gone before us charting the path of courageous dependence. His life, death, and resurrection announces good news to people who grow weary and waver in a hard world. Hold fast to him!

HOPE-FILLED REALISM

Most important, we wait on and trust in the One who faithfully walks with us, behind us, beside us, and ahead of us. The love of Jesus instills in his people an everlasting hope, and that hope empowers us to endure even the most difficult of challenges. And because our hope comes from Jesus, we find courage when looking forward by the light of his merciful control of our lives. By his truth and grace, Jesus gives us a new outlook on life, hope, and endurance.

You've likely heard about two kinds of people: optimists and pessimists. One kind sees the glass half full. The optimist wears rose-colored glasses and struggles to see the negative aspects of life. Another kind sees the glass half empty. The pessimist looks on the dark side of life, spotting trouble and expecting the worst. Most of my life, I thought the optimist and the pessimist were the only two kinds of people out there. Of the two, I fit best into the optimistic crowd.

But I wondered along the way, does God highlight one over the other? Considering the significant attention given to how God's people should view the world and their place in it, I realized a third kind of outlook exists: hope-filled realism.

Realism stands in the gap between optimism and pessimism. As the term suggests, realism looks objectively at the world. Realism takes in both the bad and the good of life in the world. The Bible makes realism uniquely Christian. Scripture gives a realistic worldview to those who trust their words. So Christians are able to face and embrace the fallen reality of sin. And though the hard state of the world can provoke despair, God has made his people uniquely fit to face life without fretting, fear, and fighting. They know they live in the best of all possible worlds, although horrible things happen within it, because God is full of grace and perfectly in control.

So the outlook of Christianity is not a sterile realism, but a hope-filled realism. And this lens on the world gives us the ultimate reason to endure. We know that in his great mercy, God "has caused us to be born again to a living hope through the resurrection of Jesus Christ from the dead, to an inheritance that is imperishable, undefiled, and unfading, kept in heaven for you" (1 Peter 1:3–4). We know that "goodness and mercy shall follow me all the days of my life" (Psalm 23:6). We know that "the sufferings of this present time are not worth comparing with the glory that is to be revealed to us" (Romans 8:18). We know that "our citizenship is in heaven, and from it we await a Savior, the Lord Jesus Christ" (Philippians 3:20). We look at the real world with hope because our King remains sovereign, wise, and good. We bank on this truth, knowing that nothing in all creation can hinder the good plans of our faithful Father.

The enduring motto *post tenebras lux* strengthens our endurance by directing our attention forward to the light of our faithful Father and our ultimate, future, final redemption in his kingdom. As hope-filled realists, we endure the hardships of today for two big reasons that we need to keep central to our lives: We know our great God performs marvelous work in the unseen realities of life, even in the midst of dark and overwhelming trials. And we can courageously depend on God because we look forward to the perfect peace of our final home in heaven. We rejoice with the apostle Peter, whose words encourage us:

> In this you rejoice, though now for a little while, if necessary, you have been grieved by various trials, so that the tested genuineness of your faith—more precious than gold that perishes though it is tested by fire—may be found to result in praise, glory, and honor at the revelation of Jesus Christ. Though you have not seen him, you love him. Though you do not now see him, you believe in him and rejoice with joy that is inexpressible and filled with glory, obtaining the outcome of your faith, the salvation of your souls. (1 Peter 1:6–9)

While escape looks away, courageous dependence can look forward with joy inexpressible. May this better way characterize your life and mine more and more every day!

QUESTIONS FOR REFLECTION

1. Do you interpret what is seen in light of the unseen, spiritual reality? We all struggle in this area. List a few examples of moments when you didn't pay attention to the unseen reality.

2. How does living with a strong focus on the seen reality lead us to escape?

3. How does living with a strong focus on the unseen reality help us to endure trials and temptations through dependence on Christ?

4. Are you more of an optimist or a pessimist? In what specific ways can you grow in hope-filled realism by repenting, believing, and obeying?

PERSONAL APPLICATION

Grab a journal and start a providence record. Make a list of all the ways God has held you fast during times of darkness. List specific passages, prayers, or biblical images that God has used to help you draw near to him when you have longed for escape.

ENDNOTES

Chapter 1

1. Thomas Watson, *The Doctrine of Repentance* (Carlisle, PA: Banner of Truth, 1988), 18.

2. Matthew Henry, *The Miniature Commentary: Being Short Comments on Every Chapter of the Holy Bible* (London: The Religious Tract Society, 1840), 422.

Chapter 2

1. Charles Spurgeon, "Comfort for the Tempted," sermon, Metropolitan Tabernacle, Newington, UK, September 27, 1883; accessed November 27, 2021, https://archive.spurgeon.org/sermons/2603.php.

2. Jodi Picoult, *My Sister's Keeper: A Novel* (United Kingdom: Simon & Schuster, 2009), 189.

3. John Bunyan and Craig John Lovik, *The Pilgrim's Progress: From This World to That Which Is to Come*, updated version (Wheaton, IL: Crossway Books, 2009), 163.

4. Jerry Bridges, *Trusting God* (Colorado Springs, CO: NavPress, 2016), 209.

Chapter 3

1. Susannah Spurgeon, *A Carillon of Bells: To Ring Out the Old Truths of Free Grace and Dying Love* (London: Passmore and Alabaster, 1896), 96.

2. Charles Spurgeon, "Divine Sovereignty," sermon, New Park Street Chapel, Southwark, May 4, 1856; accessed April 5, 2022, https://archive.spurgeon.org/sermons/0077.php.

3. Charles Spurgeon, "The Statue of David for the Sharing of the Spoil," sermon, Metropolitan Tabernacle, Newington, June

7, 1891; accessed April 5, 2022, https://archive.spurgeon.org/ser-
mons/2208.php.

Chapter 4

1. Ohio Opioid Education Alliance, "Ohio Opioid Education
Alliance Launches New PSA Campaign," accessed Sept 12, 2020,
https://dontliveindenial.org/ohio-opioid-education-alliance-
launches-new-psa-campaign/.

2. Guilherme Radaeli, "5 Easy Tests You Can Do at Home to
Tell If Your Gold Jewelry Is Fake," ToughNickel, April 18, 2020,
https://toughnickel.com/personal-finance/5-Easy-Ways-To-Tell-
If-Your-Gold-Jewelry-Is-Fake.

3. John Flavel, *Preparation for Suffering* (Forest, VA: Corner Pillar
Press, 2011), 6:9–10.

4. John Piper, *Desiring God: Meditations of a Christian Hedonist*
(Colorado Springs, CO: Multnomah, 2001), 10.

5. Stephen E. Ambrose, *Band of Brothers* (New York: Simon &
Schuster, 2001), 289.

6. Andrew Neher, *The Psychology of Transcendence*, 2nd ed. (New
York: Dover, 1990), 71.

7. Dane Ortlund, *Gentle and Lowly: The Heart of Christ for Sinners
and Sufferers* (Wheaton, IL: Crossway, 2020), 50.

Chapter 5

1. AFP, "Taiwanese Man Dies after Internet Gaming Binge,"
Bankok Post, January 17, 2015, https://www.bangkokpost.com/
world/457545/taiwanese-man-dies-after-internet-gaming-binge.

2. John Calvin, *Institutes of the Christian Religion*, 1.11.8.

3. J. B Phillips, *Your God Is Too Small: A Guide for Believers and
Skeptics Alike* (New York: Touchstone, 2004), 35.

4. Edward Mote, "My Hope Is Built On Nothing Less," hymn, 1834.

5. John Mark Comer, *The Ruthless Elimination of Hurry* (Colorado
Springs, CO: WaterBrook, 2019), 20.

6. Every time I read this passage, the words of a mentor come to
mind. Max Appel, a giant of the faith in my life, repeated to me

this advice: "We need to slow down, slow down, slow down, and spend time at the feet of the Master."

7. Timothy S. Lane and Paul David Tripp, *How People Change* (Greensboro, NC: New Growth Press, 2008).

Chapter 6

1. The story of Brenda and Eddie is adapted from Billy Joel's song "Scenes from an Italian Restaurant," *The Stranger* (Columbia Records, 1977).

2. I borrowed the concepts of peace-faking and peace-breaking from Ken Sande, author of *The Peacemaker* (among other helpful books and resources).

3. Joni Eareckson Tada, *Joni: An Unforgettable Story* (Grand Rapids: Zondervan, 1997), 149.

Chapter 7

1. World Health Organization, June 17, 2021, https://www.who.int/news-room/fact-sheets/detail/suicide.

2. Francis Thompson, *The Hound of Heaven* (London: Burns Oates & Washbourne, 1928).

3. John Newton (1725–1807) was an English hymn writer, theologian, and Anglican priest, most famous for penning the words of "Amazing Grace."

4. Iain Murray, "William Cowper and His Affliction," *The Banner of Truth*, no. 96 (September 1971): 19.

5. Carl F. H. Henry, quotes in Lewis Drummond, *Spurgeon: Prince of Preachers,* 3rd ed. (Grand Rapids, MI: Kregel, 1992), 11.

6. Zach Eswine, *Spurgeon's Sorrows* (Christian Focus, 2014).

7. C. H. Spurgeon, *Morning and Evening* (New York: Sheldon and Company, 1865), 96.

8. *Every Day with Jesus: Treasures from the Greatest Christian Writers of All Time* (Brentwood, TN: Worthy Publishing, 2011), October 9, Joni Eareckson Tada.

9. Joni Eareckson Tada, *Finding God in Hidden Places: His Presence in the Pieces of Our Lives* (Eugene, OR: Harvest House, 2020), 28.

Made in the USA
Middletown, DE
04 July 2015